Geir Helgemo, of Norway, is currently rated by many as the best player in the world. As a junior he won the European Junior Teams, the World Junior Pairs, and was runner-up in the world junior championship. At the age of only 23 he finished runner-up in the Bermuda Bowl. Only 30 now, he has won the Generali world individual championship, the Schiphol Teams, the Politiken World Pairs, the Cap Gemini Invitational and the Macallan Invitational (twice). In the USA he has won the North American Swiss teams, the North American Open Pairs, the North American Point-a-board and the Reisinger trophy (twice).

In this intriguing book Geir joins forces with Britain's top bridge writer, David Bird, to share the secrets of his amazing success. The hands feature Geir at the table, competing in tournaments around the world. Many are drawn from his private records and have not appeared before. Foremost among Geir's many qualities is imagination - the ability to conjure tricks in an unusual way. By reading this book, the aspiring player cannot help but improve his or her own game.

Other books published by Finesse Bridge Publications

by David Bird

Having Nun, Partner?

Enjoy the hilarious adventures of the bridge-playing nuns of St Hilda's Convent. The novices live in fear of the 82-year-old Mother of Discipline, dreading the appearance of her punishment book. Meanwhile, the first team (the Mother Superior, Sister Thomas, the Mother of Discipline and Sister Grace) play matches and tournaments against a range of colourful opponents.

by Marc Smith

Bridge Cardplay – Attack and Defence

Are you tired of finishing second or third? If you could make even one extra contract per session, or beat the opponents' games just a little more often, those few additional matchpoints or IMPs would elevate you into a regular winner. Give your cardplay that extra bite by adopting the techniques described in Marc Smith's latest work.

by Martin Hoffman and Marc Smith

Over Hoffman's Shoulder (to be published in February 2001)

Fabled cardplayer Martin Hoffman has achieved great success in tournaments around the world, often playing as a professional with a client across the table. How does he do it? In this exciting book he joins with Marc Smith to tell the reader exactly what went through his mind as he tackled fifty great deals - from the initial bidding, right through to their triumphant conclusion.

Bridge with Imagination

David Bird & Geir Helgemo

Finesse Bridge Publications

First published in the UK by Finesse Bridge Books Ltd 2000

ISBN 0 9538737 1 4

Distribution:

Worldwide (except USA): Central Books Ltd, 99 Wallis Road, London, E9 5LN.
Tel +44 (0)20 8986 4854.   Fax +44 (0)20 8533 5821.
E-mail orders@Centralbooks.com

USA: Baron Barclay Bridge Supplies, 3600 Chamberlain Lane #230, Louisville,
KY40241, USA.   Web site http://www.baronbarclay.com
Tel 1-800-274-2221 (Toll free) or (502) 426 - 0410. Fax (502) 426 - 2044.

For all other enquiries, please contact the publishers, Finesse Bridge Books Ltd,
69 Masbro Road, Kensington, London W14 0LS.
Fax +44 (0)20 7371 1477. E-mail finesse@bcmchess.co.uk
Web site http://www.finessebooks.com

Typeset by Ruth Edmondson
Cover design by Ian Wileman, photograph by Steven Wood
Printed in Great Britain by Redwood Books, Trowbridge, Wiltshire (UK).

Contents

Declarer Play

1. Imaginative Deception   7

2. Imagining Bad Breaks   17

3. Imaginative Creation of Entries   28

4. Imaginative Throw-Ins   32

5. Imagination in the Trump Suit   52

6. Imaginative Play in a 4-3 Fit   67

7. Imagining the Hidden Hands   73

8. Imaginative Destruction of Entries   92

9. Imaginative Squeezes   97

Defence

10. Imaginative Switches   112

11. Imagination in the Second Seat   126

12. Imaginative Drawing of Trumps in Defence   129

13. Imaginative Defence in the Endgame   133

14. Imagination in the Third Seat   139

15. Imaginative Communications Play in Defence   143

16. Imaginative Deception in Defence   150

Many thanks to David Gostyn for his most
helpful review of the proofs for this book.

1
Imaginative Deception

Defence is difficult and defenders make mistakes! Give them a chance to go wrong and they will often take it. Even when a contract looks hopeless, don't give up. There are two other players at the table who may be willing to help you.

Geir solicited the defenders' assistance on this deal, from the 1999 Reisinger win in Boston.

East-West Game
Dealer North

	♠ A K 7 5	
	♡ 6 3	
	◊ A J 3 2	
	♣ 8 7 5	

♠ Q 10 2		♠ —
♡ K Q J 9		♡ 10 8 5 2
◊ 5	N W E S	◊ K Q 8 7 4
♣ Q J 10 6 4		♣ A K 9 2

	♠ J 9 8 6 4 3	
	♡ A 7 4	
	◊ 10 9 6	
	♣ 3	

West	North **Forrester**	East	South **Helgemo**
-	1◊	pass	1♠
pass	2♠	pass	3♠
all pass			

Geir's 3♠ was not a game try. His partner had shown a lower-range opening bid with length in both diamonds and spades. It was clear, therefore, that East-West would have a good contract available in one of the other suits. If South has passed 2♠, West might well have protected with a double, allowing his side to reach their cold game in hearts. West led the king of hearts against 3♠. How would you have played the contract?

Geir ducked the heart lead and won the heart continuation with the ace. His next move was to lead the jack of trumps! He had no intention of running this card, of course. His aim was to tempt a cover, should West hold all three trumps. West duly covered with the queen, taken by dummy's ace. East showed out and Geir eventually returned to his hand with a club ruff to finesse against ♠10. Nine tricks resulted.

Did West have any excuse for covering with the queen? None at all! In theory it might save a trick if South held four trumps to the jack and East held 9-x. Declarer would not lead the jack from such a holding, of course. He would cash the ace and king, hoping for the queen to fall.

There are several similar positions where you can tempt the defenders to cover in the trump suit.

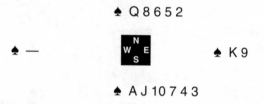

Cross to dummy and lead the queen. East shouldn't cover but half the world's defenders will do.

You can take advantage of such a tendency in this position too:

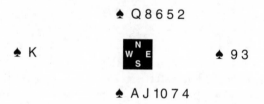

Again you lead ♠Q from the table. If East is a defender who would usually cover with the king, play for the drop when he produces a low card!

Geir was at the helm of the next contract, also from the 1999 Reisinger.

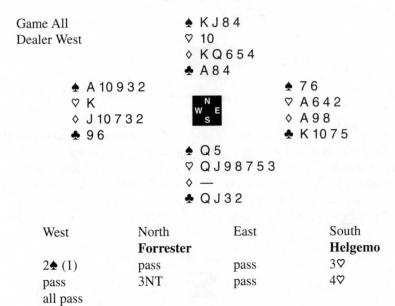

Game All   ♠ K J 8 4
Dealer West   ♡ 10
              ◊ K Q 6 5 4
              ♣ A 8 4

♠ A 10 9 3 2   ♠ 7 6
♡ K   ♡ A 6 4 2
◊ J 10 7 3 2   ◊ A 9 8
♣ 9 6   ♣ K 10 7 5

              ♠ Q 5
              ♡ Q J 9 8 7 5 3
              ◊ —
              ♣ Q J 3 2

West	North	East	South
	Forrester		**Helgemo**
2♠ (1)	pass	pass	3♡
pass	3NT	pass	4♡
all pass			

(1) Weak two bid, 5-9 points and five or six spades.

West led ◊J, which was covered by the king and ace and ruffed in the South hand. Suppose you had been the declarer. What would you have done next?

Some players would have led ♣Q, hoping to lose just one spade trick and two trumps. It's not a good shot. If West has six spades for his weak two you may suffer an immediate ruff. In any case you can't take your discards before drawing trumps. West will switch to a club when he takes his trump honour, so you would surely need the king of clubs onside.

Geir tried something different. At Trick 2 he led ♣5. West duly read this as a singleton and played low, hoping to present declarer with a guess. Geir rose with dummy's king of spades and threw his remaining spade on the queen of diamonds. Still needing to escape for only one club loser, he made good use of the entry to dummy by playing a club to the queen. Subsequently he was able to play ace and another club, making the contract for the loss of just two trumps and a club. South had made the lesser contract of 3♡ at the other table, so a full board rested on the success of the heart game.

Geir's intention on that deal was to make it look as if he had a finesse to take in the spade suit. The technique can be used in various situations:

◊ J 10 4 3

◊ Q 9 7 5 ◊ A 8 6 2

◊ K

If you hope to avoid a loser in this side suit, your best chance is to lead the jack from dummy. East may play low, expecting you to run the card to his partner's queen. Prospects are nowhere near so good if you lead a low card from dummy instead. East is likely to rise with the ace – a play that will gain when declarer holds a singleton king or queen.

Sometimes you want to disguise the fact that you have a finesse to take:

◊ K 10 7 6 2

◊ A 9 4 3 ◊ Q 8

◊ J 5

You are playing in 6♠, let's suppose, and all depends on making the right guess in this side suit. Your best shot may be to lead ◊5 early in the play. If West fears the card is a singleton (and you have another potential loser elsewhere), he may rise with the ace. Should he not do so, you would place the ace with East and finesse dummy's 10. If you lead the jack instead, West will be aware that you have a guess to make in the suit. Even if the jack is singleton, you may choose to run it to East's queen.

During the 1997 Bermuda Bowl, played in Tunisia's Hammamet, Geir himself fell victim to an imaginative deception. He and Tor Helness faced the American maestros, Jeff Meckstroth and Eric Rodwell.

Game All   ♠ A 9 8
Dealer North   ♡ J 10 6 5 2
                     ◊ A 10 2
                     ♣ K 8

♠ K 7 5 3		♠ Q J 6 2
♡ K 8	N	♡ A 9 7 4
◊ K J 9 7 4	W E	◊ Q 8 6 3
♣ 3 2	S	♣ Q

                   ♠ 10 4
                   ♡ Q 3
                   ◊ 5
                   ♣ A J 10 9 7 6 5 4

West	North	East	South
Helness	**Rodwell**	**Helgemo**	**Meckstroth**
-	1♡	pass	3♣
pass	3NT	pass	4♣
pass	5♣	all pass	

Meckstroth's 3♣ response was weak and non-forcing, but Rodwell could see a fair prospect of running nine tricks in notrumps (just as he would if South had opened a vulnerable 3♣). 3NT on a mere 19 points cannot be beaten and was duly bid and made by the Norwegian North-South at the other table. Playing a strong club system, Meckstroth knew that his partner could not hold more than 15 points. He decided to pull 3NT to 4♣ and arrived in the seemingly hopeless club game.

Helness led ◊4 (third and fifth leads) and Meckstroth called for dummy's 10! This was a cost-nothing deception, since his spade loser could subsequently be thrown on the diamond ace. Geir won with the diamond queen and, unable to read the diamond situation, returned a second round of the suit. Meckstroth discarded a heart and won with dummy's ace of diamonds.

When a low heart was led from dummy now, there was no defence. If Geir rose with the ace, his partner's king of hearts would subsequently be ruffed out. He chose instead to duck and Helness won the bare queen with the king. Nothing could prevent declarer from taking a ruffing finesse against the ace of hearts and eleven tricks were made.

That same year, 1997, Geir partnered Geir Olav Tislevoll in the European Open Pairs. At one stage they faced the possibility of a zero board on this deal:

East-West Game
Dealer West

	♠ J 10 7		
	♡ 5 2		
	◊ J 10 3		
	♣ Q 10 9 8 7		

♠ A 8 6 4 2		♠ K Q 5 3
♡ A K 8	N	♡ 7 6 4 3
◊ Q 9	W E	◊ A 6
♣ 6 5 3	S	♣ A 4 2

♠ 9
♡ Q J 10 9
◊ K 8 7 5 4 2
♣ K J

West	North	East	South
Olanski	**Tislevoll**	**Starkowski**	**Helgemo**
1♠	pass	2♣	2◊
pass	3◊	4♠	5◊
double	all pass		

West led the ace of hearts, Geir dropping the 10, then switched to ◊9, won by East's ace. Another trump was returned and Geir had his first problem. If he misguessed in the trump suit, the defenders would be able to pick up 800, merely by cashing their top cards. How did the trump suit lie?

Geir cast his mind back to the bidding. If West held only one diamond, he would surely not have passed on the second round. According to his shape he would have rebid 2♠ or 2♡, or raised his partner's clubs. Concluding that West must hold two trumps, Geir rose with the king of trumps. West's queen of trumps appeared and the spectre of an 800 in the minus column had been dismissed.

Geir next led ♡9. West chose not to rise with the king and the penalty had now been reduced to 300! West had no excuse for this lapse, of course, but it is worth remembering that defenders are less likely to cover when you play the lower or lowest card from equals. Had the queen been led, the most somnolent of Wests would have produced the king.

Tor Helness made a similar play on this deal from the Norway-Sweden match in the 1993 European Championship:

North-South Game
Dealer East

♠ 6 5 3
♡ J 7 6 5
♢ 9 8 5 2
♣ 9 5

♠ J 8 2
♡ K Q 9 2
♢ K Q 6 3
♣ 7 3

```
  N
W   E
  S
```

♠ Q 7
♡ A 4
♢ A J 10 7 4
♣ 10 8 4 2

♠ A K 10 9 4
♡ 10 8 3
♢ —
♣ A K Q J 6

West	North	East	South
Brunzell	**Helgemo**	**Nielsen**	**Helness**
-	-	1NT	double
redouble	2♣	double	pass
pass	redouble	pass	4♠
double	all pass		

The Danish East opened with a weak 1NT. When Helness doubled, West redoubled to show a strong hand. Geir now bid 2♣ in the hope that a double would permit a subsequent redouble for rescue. This all came to pass, except that – much to Geir's surprise – Helness rescued at the four level!

When Brunzell led the king of hearts his partner should surely have overtaken with the ace and returned the suit. It was not as if it might cost a trick, should he use his ♠Q7 for ruffing. He chose to play low instead and West continued with a second heart to the bare ace.

Helness won the trump switch and drew a second round with the king. He now needed three rounds of clubs to stand up, in order to dispose of two hearts from dummy. To aid his prospects, he cashed the ace and king of clubs, then continued with the jack. Uncertain as to the position of the club queen, the Swedish West declined to ruff with his master trump. Curtains! A heart was thrown from dummy and another went on the club queen, as West ruffed. The defenders scored just two hearts and one trump and the contract was made.

Many players never think of such deceptive plays, or – worse – don't consider them worthwhile. 'A good defender would never fall for it,' they say. This attitude costs a bundle of tricks in the long run. Give the opponents a chance to go wrong and they are often willing to take it.

West could not wait to grab such an opportunity on the next deal, played by Geir in the 1995 Trondheim Open. In the main pairs event he was partnered by Jan Olav Røseng.

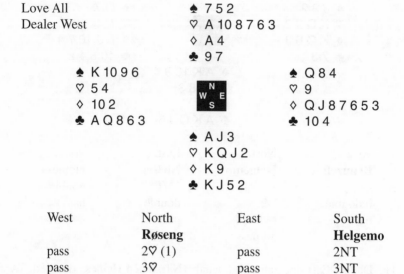

Love All
Dealer West

♠ 7 5 2
♥ A 10 8 7 6 3
♦ A 4
♣ 9 7

♠ K 10 9 6
♥ 5 4
♦ 10 2
♣ A Q 8 6 3

♠ Q 8 4
♥ 9
♦ Q J 8 7 6 5 3
♣ 10 4

♠ A J 3
♥ K Q J 2
♦ K 9
♣ K J 5 2

West	North **Røseng**	East	South **Helgemo**
pass	2♥ (1)	pass	2NT
pass	3♥	pass	3NT
all pass			

(1) Weak two bid, 5-9 points and usually six hearts.

Geir's 2NT asked partner if he held any side-suit singleton. The 3♥ response denied a singleton, suggesting 6-3-2-2 shape. Geir elected to play in 3NT, rather than the heart game, and West led ♣6 to his partner's 10.

Ten tricks were on view but it was by no means clear how this could be bumped to eleven. Geir tried the effect of winning East's ♣10 with the king! At Trick 2 he continued innocently with a low club towards dummy. West could scarcely believe this lapse by a player who was supposed to have a good reputation. He won with the queen of clubs and smartly cashed the club ace. He was disappointed to see his partner show out on this trick and Geir could now claim eleven tricks.

Most of the matchpoints had been won in the auction, by the decision to play in notrumps. The second overtrick gained only two extra matchpoints, but – as it happens – Geir and his partner went on to win the event by just one matchpoint.

On the next deal, from the 1998 Reisinger, Geir made a similar play in the club suit. His aim on this occasion was to feign weakness in the suit, drawing attention from a hole in his armour elsewhere.

North-South Game	♠ J 8 7 4 2	
Dealer East	♡ Q J 4	
	◇ 9 2	
	♣ A 3 2	

♠ 9 3		♠ 10 6 5
♡ A 7 3	N W E S	♡ 9 5 2
◇ K 10 4		◇ A J 8 6 5
♣ Q 10 9 8 7		♣ 6 5

	♠ A K Q
	♡ K 10 8 6
	◇ Q 7 3
	♣ K J 4

West	North	East	South
	Forrester		**Helgemo**
-	-	pass	1♣
pass	1♠	pass	2NT
pass	3NT	all pass	

West led ♣10 and Geir could count a likely eight top tricks. If he won with the jack and led a heart, there was an evident risk that the defenders might grab the ace immediately and cash at least four diamond tricks.

Hoping to encourage the defenders to persist with clubs when they gained the lead, Geir won the first club trick with the king! He then played a heart to the queen, which won the trick.

Since a club trick had been sacrificed, declarer had only eight tricks and could not run for home at this stage. In any case, the Reisinger is scored at point-a-board (pairs scoring for two tables: one point for a win, half a point for a draw). North-South at the other table were likely to have recorded +620 in spades, so a humble +600 would not win the board. Geir persisted with the four of hearts to the king (he could not afford to lead the jack of hearts, because this might be needed to untangle the spades). West won with the heart ace and – yes! – played the queen of clubs. The jack of clubs was transformed into a winner again and the communications were present to score all the major-suit winners. Geir's +660 beat the +620 (as predicted) from the other table.

Apart from the deception in clubs, note how important it was to keep the powerful spades under wraps. It was difficult indeed for West to visualize that a diamond switch was needed.

West found it difficult to read the diamond position on the next deal too, from a 1996 pairs event in Trondheim, Norway. Geir's partner was Bjørn Olav Ekren.

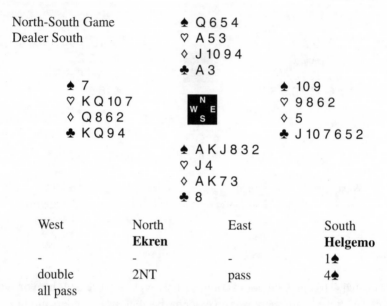

North-South Game
Dealer South

```
              ♠ Q 6 5 4
              ♡ A 5 3
              ◊ J 10 9 4
              ♣ A 3
♠ 7                          ♠ 10 9
♡ K Q 10 7                   ♡ 9 8 6 2
◊ Q 8 6 2        N           ◊ 5
♣ K Q 9 4      W   E         ♣ J 10 7 6 5 2
                 S
              ♠ A K J 8 3 2
              ♡ J 4
              ◊ A K 7 3
              ♣ 8
```

West	North	East	South
	Ekren		**Helgemo**
-	-	-	1♠
double	2NT	pass	4♠
all pass			

West led ♡K, won in the dummy, and Geir drew trumps in two rounds. Eleven tricks were guaranteed but what was the best chance of a twelfth?

West's double suggested that he would hold at least three diamonds to the queen, so at Trick 4 Geir led a low diamond towards the dummy! West played low, not overjoyed to see dummy's jack win the trick. Geir returned to the ace of diamonds, discovering that West had started with four cards in the suit. No matter. When the trump suit was run West had to reduce to ♡Q ◊Q8. He was then thrown in with a heart to lead away from the queen of diamonds. Plus 680 was good for almost all the matchpoints.

Should West have fallen for this deception? Certainly not. The bidding marked South with at least one of the top diamond honours. Holding A-x-x or K-x-x, he would surely have led the suit from the dummy, finessing East for the queen. Only if he held both diamond honours, would declarer be able to read West for the queen, leading the suit from hand.

2
Imagining Bad Breaks

A bad break comes to light and you sit back in your chair, wondering what you can do about it. Often it will be too late! You needed to foresee the bad break before it became apparent and then take steps to counter it.

On this deal from the 1999 Norwegian Premier League Geir sat South, partnering Per Erik Austberg:

Love All
Dealer West

	♠ K Q 10	
	♡ K Q 4 2	
	◇ A	
	♣ A Q 9 7 6	

♠ 9 7		♠ J 8 5 3
♡ 7 6	N W E S	♡ 10 9 8
◇ Q 9 6 5		◇ K J 10 3 2
♣ K J 10 3 2		♣ 5

	♠ A 6 4 2	
	♡ A J 5 3	
	◇ 8 7 4	
	♣ 8 4	

West	North	East	South
	Austberg		**Helgemo**
pass	1♣	pass	1♡
pass	3◇	pass	3♠
pass	4NT	pass	5♡
pass	6♡	all pass	

North's 3◇ was a splinter bid, agreeing hearts as trumps and showing at most one diamond. Although Geir held only nine points facing a one-bid, his diamond holding was ideal facing shortage and he did hold two aces. He cue-bid the spade control and was soon in a heart slam. How would you have played this contract on a trump lead?

Geir won the trump lead in the South hand and immediately took a club finesse, which won. What next? If you draw trumps you will still need some further luck, even if trumps are 3-2. One of the black suits will have to break evenly.

Geir aimed to set up the North hand, even if the black suits were both splitting poorly. His next move was an imaginative one – he played a low club from both hands! West won with the 10 and played another trump, won with the king. Geir could not now be prevented from ruffing two clubs in the South hand and drawing the last trump. Count the tricks he made: three spades, one diamond, two clubs, four trump tricks and two ruffs in the South hand. Twelve in all.

Suppose declarer is careless and plays the ace of clubs at Trick 3. East will ruff and play a second round of trumps. Declarer will then have only two trumps left to deal with three losers (whether he takes his ruffs in the North hand or the South hand). The spade suit provides only three tricks and that is one down. This is an example of the situation we mentioned at the start the chapter. It is too late to make a plan once East has ruffed the ace of clubs. You must foresee a 5-1 club break and determine a counter to it.

The scene switches to a 1999 pairs tournament in Sandefjord. This time a bad break in diamonds is declarer's main concern.

Love All	♠ Q J	
Dealer North	♡ A K 10 9 8	
	◊ Q J 8 5 4 2	
	♣ —	

♠ 9 3		♠ 8 7 6 5 2
♡ J	N W E S	♡ Q 7 6 4 3
◊ A 10 9 7 3		◊ —
♣ J 10 8 5 4		♣ 7 3 2

♠ A K 10 4	
♡ 5 2	
◊ K 6	
♣ A K Q 9 6	

West	North	East	South
	Austberg		**Helgemo**
-	1◊	pass	2♣
pass	2♡	pass	2♠
pass	3♡	pass	6NT
all pass			

Seeking a safe lead, West reached for ♣J. Since three diamond tricks would be enough for the contract, Geir discarded a diamond from dummy and won the trick with the ace. Suppose you had been playing the hand. What would you have done next?

It would be a mistake to lead the king of diamonds, since if West held a singleton ace this would promote a second diamond trick for East's 10-9-7-3. Geir duly led ◊6. If West played his ace on thin air, declarer would have the three diamond tricks he needed. West played low and dummy's queen won the trick, East showing out. The best remaining chance was that West held a singleton or doubleton heart honour. When Geir cashed ♡A. the jack fell on his left. Yes! He continued with king and another heart, forcing out East's queen, and then had twelve tricks – four spades, four hearts, one diamond and three clubs.

Another declarer found the same Morton's Fork in diamonds but sadly for him he had discarded a heart at Trick 1! He was able to establish only three heart tricks, not the four that he needed.

What would have happened if West had held a small singleton heart, showing out on the second round of the suit? Declarer can come very close to an endplay on West and an interesting end position arises. The plays starts in the same way: club to the ace, diamond to the queen, ace and king of hearts. When West shows out on the second heart, declarer plays four rounds of spades. West must retain his club guard and two diamonds. Declarer cashes one more top club, throwing dummy's last heart, and this end position has been reached:

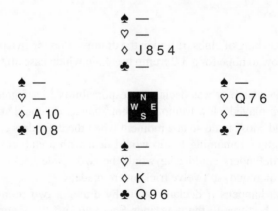

Declarer plays the king of diamonds. If West captures, he will have to surrender the last three tricks, either to declarer or the dummy. Instead, West underplays with the 10! Now declarer has to give him a club and a diamond for one down.

On the next deal, from a 1996 inter-club match, a bad trump break was Geir's main concern. He was partnered by Rolf Allander:

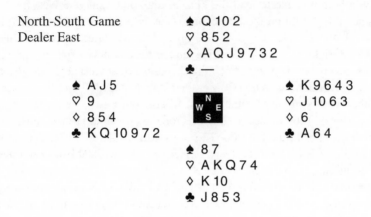

North-South Game
Dealer East

	♠ Q 10 2		
	♡ 8 5 2		
	◊ A Q J 9 7 3 2		
	♣ —		
♠ A J 5		♠ K 9 6 4 3	
♡ 9		♡ J 10 6 3	
◊ 8 5 4		◊ 6	
♣ K Q 10 9 7 2		♣ A 6 4	
	♠ 8 7		
	♡ A K Q 7 4		
	◊ K 10		
	♣ J 8 5 3		

West	North **Allander**	East	South **Helgemo**
-	-	pass	1♡
2♣	2◊	3♣	pass
pass	3♡	pass	4♡
all pass			

West led the king of clubs, ruffed in the dummy. Playing in a pairs, it would be tempting now to hope for a 3-2 trump break, in which case all thirteen tricks can be made.

In an IMPs match, it was declarer's responsibility to safeguard the game. At Trick 2 Geir played a low trump from both hands. He could afford to lose a trump trick and chose to do so at a moment when the defenders could cause no damage. Dummy's remaining trump would deal with a club continuation, so the most the defenders could take would be two spade tricks. West in fact switched to a diamond, so twelve tricks were made.

Look what happens if declarer starts by drawing two rounds of trumps instead. When he turns to the diamonds East will ruff the second round and there will be no protection in the club suit. The game will go three down. Strange but true is the fact that an unlikely diamond lead would defeat four hearts. If declarer ducks the first round of trumps West can win and give his partner a diamond ruff. If instead declarer plays ace and another trump, East can force dummy's last trump with a club switch, causing insoluble entry problems.

We move now to the 1997 Cavendish Pairs, a cross-IMPed event played in Las Vegas. Geir received a friendly lead on this deal but still had to calculate accurately how to play the trump suit:

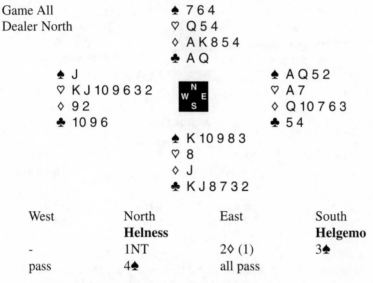

Game All
Dealer North

	West	North **Helness**	East	South **Helgemo**
	-	1NT	2◊ (1)	3♠
	pass	4♠	all pass	

(1) Diamonds and an unspecified major.

West led ◊9, Geir cashing two rounds of the suit to dispose of his heart loser. All now depended on how he tackled the trump suit. What would your play have been?

If a trump to the ten loses to a singleton queen or jack, declarer will lose control. West will force the South hand with a heart. When declarer crosses to a club and leads a second round of trumps, East will rise with the ace and force South again. The contract will go at least one down.

Aware of this, Geir made the percentage play of a trump to the king. This line would fail only if West held a singleton ace of trumps (or an insurmountable A-Q-J-5). When the trump jack fell under the king, Geir abandoned the suit and ran the clubs. East scored three trump tricks but that was all.

When the trumps break badly, and cannot be picked up by finessing, it is sometimes possible to achieve an endplay in the trump suit itself. To achieve this, you usually have to read the key defender's distribution in the side suits. Such was the case on this deal from a match in the 1996 Norwegian teams championship:

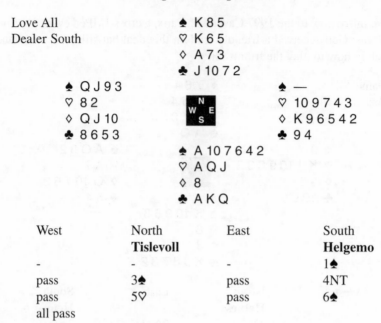

Love All
Dealer South

```
                    ♠ K 8 5
                    ♡ K 6 5
                    ◇ A 7 3
                    ♣ J 10 7 2
♠ Q J 9 3                              ♠ —
♡ 8 2                                  ♡ 10 9 7 4 3
◇ Q J 10                               ◇ K 9 6 5 4 2
♣ 8 6 5 3                              ♣ 9 4
                    ♠ A 10 7 6 4 2
                    ♡ A Q J
                    ◇ 8
                    ♣ A K Q
```

West	North	East	South
	Tislevoll		**Helgemo**
-	-	-	1♠
pass	3♠	pass	4NT
pass	5♡	pass	6♠
all pass			

West led the queen of diamonds and Geir won with dummy's ace. The only possible problem was a 4-0 trump break. Geir ruffed a diamond, West playing the jack, then led a low trump towards dummy. If a sleepy West had followed with the three, Geir would have called for dummy's five, ensuring only one trump loser. No, West was following the proceedings alertly and inserted the nine. Dummy's king won the trick and East showed out. What could be done now?

For a trump endplay to succeed, West had to be reduced to just his three remaining trumps. To cash the right cards, Geir had to determine West's shape. West would need to hold at least three clubs anyway, so the first move was to cash three rounds of that suit.

East showed out on the third round of clubs. The slam could now be made if West held 4-3-2-4 or 4-2-3-4 shape, but Geir had to guess which. If West held three hearts, the winning play would be to ruff dummy's master club; if instead he held three diamonds, declarer would have to ruff another diamond and discard a heart on the jack of clubs. Which play would you have chosen?

Geir decided to play West for three diamonds. One indication was that East has shown an even number of diamonds with his signal at Trick 1. The other was that Q-J doubleton is not such an attractive opening lead as Q-J-10 or Q-J-9. Geir cashed two rounds of hearts and threw his last heart on ♣J. He then ruffed another diamond in his hand, please to see West follow suit. This end position had been reached:

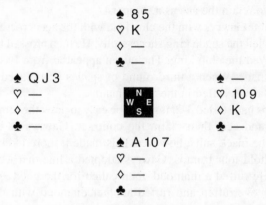

```
              ♠ 8 5
              ♡ K
              ◇ —
              ♣ —
  ♠ Q J 3              ♠ —
  ♡ —         N        ♡ 10 9
  ◇ —       W   E      ◇ K
  ♣ —         S        ♣ —
              ♠ A 10 7
              ♡ —
              ◇ —
              ♣ —
```

The hard work was at an end. It remained only to lead a low trump towards the dummy. West had to win with one honour, then lead away from the other.

Geir won the 1996 Generali Masters Individual tournament, contested in Paris, despite being on the receiving end of a fine piece of cardplay on this deal:

North-South Game
Dealer South

```
                   ♠ J 9 7 6 4
                   ♡ A Q 3
                   ◇ —
                   ♣ A K J 7 6
  ♠ Q 10 8                        ♠ 5 3
  ♡ 7             N               ♡ 10 9 8 2
  ◇ 9 8 7 2     W   E             ◇ K Q J 4 3
  ♣ 10 9 5 4 2    S               ♣ Q 8
                   ♠ A K 2
                   ♡ K J 6 5 4
                   ◇ A 10 6 5
                   ♣ 3
```

West	North	East	South
Helgemo	**Kokish**	**Westerhof**	**Gawrys**
-	-	-	1♡
pass	1♠	pass	2◇
pass	3♣	pass	4♠
pass	6♡	all pass	

Geir found the best lead of a club. On any other attack, declarer can draw trumps and set up the spades, using the club ace as an entry. (He would ruff a diamond lead, to retain the ace as a stopper.)

Poland's Piotr Gawrys won the club lead with the ace, crossed to the ace of spades, and cashed the spade king successfully. He then crossed to the queen of trumps and played the club king. The queen appeared from East and declarer threw his last spade. When a third round of spades was played, East threw a diamond and Gawrys ruffed in the South hand.

If the trumps had started 3-2, it would be easy to draw the remaining trumps with the king and ace, then claim the contract. Gawrys had noted East's doubletons in the black suits, however. This made it more likely than normal that he would hold four trumps. Gawrys adopted a line that would deal with this situation. He ruffed a diamond, then called for the good ♣J. When East ruffed, declarer overruffed and ruffed another diamond with the trump ace. These cards remained:

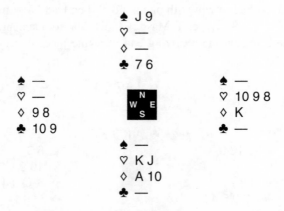

When a master spade was played, East had to ruff. Gawrys discarded his diamond loser, won the diamond return, and claimed the last two tricks with his master trumps.

On another deal from the same event (the 1996 Generali Masters) it was Geir who had to deal with a bad break:

Game All   ♠ A Q 9
Dealer South   ♡ 10 8 4 3
                  ◊ 4 3 2
                  ♣ A K 6

♠ J 8 3 2		♠ 10 7 6 4
♡ 9 7 5	N	♡ A K 2
◊ Q J	W E	◊ 10 9 8 6 5
♣ Q J 10 5	S	♣ 7

                  ♠ K 5
                  ♡ Q J 6
                  ◊ A K 7
                  ♣ 9 8 4 3 2

West	North	East	South
Westra	**Mouiel**	**Freeman**	**Helgemo**
-	-	-	1♣
pass	1♡	pass	1NT
pass	3NT	all pass	

Holland's Berri Westra found the best lead of ◊Q. Suppose you had been the declarer. How would you have played the contract?

There are seven top tricks and if you look only at the heart and club suits, ignoring the context of the whole hand, you would choose to play on hearts to seek the two extra tricks you need. By leading twice towards the Q-J, you score two heart tricks 81% of the time. This is better odds than finding a 3-2 break in clubs (68%). The entry situation does not permit playing hearts to best advantage, however, and there would also be some risk of losing three diamonds and two hearts. It is therefore better to play on clubs rather than hearts.

Some declarers won the diamond lead and played the ace and king of clubs. When the bad break came to light, they switched to hearts. East rose with the king and played another diamond. Declarer could not duck this trick or West would gain the lead and cash his club winners. When the second diamond was captured, however, East was able to win the next heart and cash the contract one down.

Geir won the diamond lead and also decided to play on clubs. What if the suit was 4-1? Could anything be done? The situation would clearly be hopeless if West held a singleton club. What if East held a singleton queen, jack or 10? The ace would drop the singleton but West's remaining cards would be good enough to deal with declarer's 9-8-4. The only singleton that declarer could handle was single seven with East!

At Trick 2 Geir led ♣8 from his hand. West played low and so did the dummy. As if at a conjurer's behest, the ♣7 appeared from East. Geir could now have scored four club tricks, for a safe total of nine. In fact he crossed to ♣A and took the risk of playing on hearts. East rose with the king and played another diamond. West's bare jack was allowed to win and Geir could now set up the heart suit, scoring an overtrick for a joint top.

We will end the chapter with a hand that offered potential for humour. It arose in the final of the 1993 World Junior Championships. Norway faced Germany and Geir's partner, Lasse Aaseng, was South.

East-West Game
Dealer East

	♠ A J	
	♡ Q 10 9 8 7 6 5 3	
	◊ 10 5	
	♣ K	
♠ 3 2		♠ K 9 8 7 6 4
♡ K		♡ J 2
◊ Q J 4 3		◊ 8 7 6 2
♣ J 9 7 6 3 2		♣ 5
	♠ Q 10 5	
	♡ A 4	
	◊ A K 9	
	♣ A Q 10 8 4	

West	North	East	South
Rohowski	**Helgemo**	**Hopfenheit**	**Aaseng**
-	-	pass	2NT
pass	3◊	pass	3♡
pass	4NT	pass	5♣
pass	6♡	all pass	

Geir's 4NT was Roman Key-card Blackwood and the response showed three aces, or two aces and the king of trumps. How would you play the contract when West leads the queen of diamonds?

Declarer's only concern was to avoid two trump losers. Aaseng could see the safety play. He won the diamond lead with the ace and crossed to dummy with ♣K. He then led ♡3, playing the four from his hand when East contributed the two. (This guarded against all three trumps with East. If East had shown out on the first round, declarer would have risen with the ace and led towards dummy's queen.)

Rohowski won with the bare king of trumps and returned a second round of clubs. If Aaseng had let his concentration drop, ruffing low in the dummy, he would have found the only way to lose two trump tricks and go down! No, aware that there was only one more trump out, he ruffed with dummy's queen of trumps and claimed the remaining tricks.

Disaster avoided.

3

Imaginative Creation of Entries

Declarer is concerned with two aspects of communication. On the constructive side, he must maintain the entries that he needs to the dummy and to his own hand. On the destructive side, he must attempt to break the link between the two defenders. In the present chapter we will look at some clever moves used to promote declarer's own entry situation.

Many a contract is blown at Trick 1. This is particularly the case when entries are in short supply and you need to judge where you should win the first trick. Geir had to play carefully on this deal from the 1999 Norwegian Premier League, where his partner was Per Erik Austberg:

```
Love All              ♠ A J 10 9 7
Dealer West           ♡ A J 7 6 4
                      ◊ 5 2
                      ♣ 4

  ♠ 8 3                               ♠ Q 5
  ♡ K 9 3          N                  ♡ Q 10 8 5 2
  ◊ A K 10 9 3   W   E                ◊ Q 7
  ♣ K Q 5          S                  ♣ J 10 7 3

                      ♠ K 6 4 2
                      ♡ —
                      ◊ J 8 6 4
                      ♣ A 9 8 6 2
```

West	North	East	South
	Austberg		**Helgemo**
1NT	2♣ (1)	2♡	3♠
pass	4♠	all pass	

(1) Both majors, but could be only 4-4.

West led ♠3 and the whole hand hinged on declarer's play to the first trick. Geir's plan was to play on clubs, hoping to set up a long card in the suit. Since the king of trumps would be needed as an entry later, he rose with the trump ace. A club to the ace was followed by a club ruff and a second trump to the king. It was no surprise when East's queen appeared, since defenders rarely lead from a trump holding including the queen. (Nor do they often lead a singleton trump, although that was impossible here after West's 1NT opening.)

Geir ruffed another club, pleased to see the suit breaking 4-3, then cashed the ace of hearts, throwing a diamond. A heart ruff returned the lead to the South hand and a third club ruff established the suit. Just three diamond tricks were lost.

Go back to Trick 1 and see what happens if declarer plays the jack from dummy. East will cover with the queen and if you can find any way to make the contract after that, we will refund you the cost of this book!

We move now to the 1990 Junior European Championship, played in Neumunster, Germany. Geir was partnered by Per Arne Flatt and faced communication problems on this deal:

North-South Game	♠ J 3
Dealer South	♡ K J 8 5 4
	◊ J 9 2
	♣ 8 3 2

♠ 10 8 2		♠ K Q 9 7 5
♡ Q 9 7 6 3	**N** **W** **E** **S**	♡ 10 2
◊ —		◊ Q 8 5 3
♣ K 10 7 5 4		♣ Q J

	♠ A 6 4
	♡ A
	◊ A K 10 7 6 4
	♣ A 9 6

West	North	East	South
	Flatt		**Helgemo**
-	-	-	2♣
2NT (1)	3♡	pass	3NT
all pass			

(1) Any two-suiter

West led ♣4 and Geir allowed East's jack to win. He won the club continuation and had to decide how to tackle the diamonds. If he played the suit from the top, all would be well if the queen fell in two rounds. Indeed, he would score an overtrick. If the queen did not fall, which was more likely than normal after West's two-suited overcall, declarer would have only eight tricks. There would be no entry to the king of hearts.

Geir resolved his problem in an unusual, and brave, way. He cashed the ace of hearts at Trick 3, then led a low diamond from his hand! All was well when dummy's jack was headed by East's queen. Geir won the spade return, crossed to ◊9 to score the king of hearts, and returned to his hand with a diamond to run nine tricks.

Note that Geir could not afford to cash one high diamond before ducking a diamond. With the third round of diamonds needed to reach the heart king, a spade return would kill the re-entry card to the South hand.

Some two years later, Hervé Mouiel of France made a very similar play, facing USA in the final of the 1992 Olympiad.

Game All	♠ —		
Dealer West	♥ A K 2		
	◊ A K J 8 6 2		
	♣ 9 8 5 4		

♠ Q 8 6 5		♠ J 10 7 4
♥ Q 9 6		♥ J 10 8 5 3
◊ Q 7 3	N W E S	◊ 5
♣ A J 2		♣ Q 10 3

♠ A K 9 3 2
♥ 7 4
◊ 10 9 4
♣ K 7 6

West	North	East	South
Rodwell	**Lévy**	**Meckstroth**	**Mouiel**
pass	1◊	pass	1♠
pass	2◊	pass	3◊
pass	3♥	pass	3NT
all pass			

There's the proof. There is such a thing as an 11-point hand on which Eric Rodwell would not open the bidding!

Rodwell led ♥Q against 3NT and Mouiel won in the dummy. It is not recorded whether he was aware of Geir's play two years before. He did, however, play a diamond to the 10 next. This safety play guaranteed the contract unless East had been dealt all four diamonds (and could therefore duck the first round of the suit). West won with the diamond queen and cleared the heart suit. Mouiel could now cross to ◇9, cash two spades, and return to the ace of diamonds to run nine tricks. The diamonds were indeed 3-1, so the safety play was necessary.

We'll end the chapter with a remarkable hand. Norway faced Great Britain in the 1993 European Championship.

```
North-South Game        ♠ A Q 9 7 6 5 4
Dealer East             ♡ 5 4 2
                        ◇ —
                        ♣ Q 9 8
   ♠ K 8 3                         ♠ J 2
   ♡ J 9 7            N            ♡ 10 8 6
   ◇ 9 7          W       E        ◇ Q J 5 4 3 2
   ♣ K J 6 5 4        S            ♣ 7 3
                        ♠ 10
                        ♡ A K Q 3
                        ◇ A K 10 8 6
                        ♣ A 10 2
```

West	North	East	South
Tredinnick	**Aa**	**Tredinnick**	**Groetheim**
-	-	3◇	pass
pass	3♠	pass	4NT
pass	5◇	pass	6NT
all pass			

Glenn Groetheim passed 3◇ in the hope that partner would re-open with a double. (Some bridge players are optimists!) His partner did at least find a bid, protecting with 3♠. Groetheim now carried the bidding to 6NT. How would you have played this contract when West leads ◇9?

The slam is not exactly cold (ahem) but Groetheim spotted the only real chance. He would have to throw West on lead, forcing him to provide an entry to dummy's spades. He cashed his red-suit winners, pleased to see that West was not left with a winning heart. He then finessed ♣Q successfully, cashed ♣A, and exited with a spade. Poor Gerald Tredinnick, sitting West, had to win with the king and lead a club. With West holding both club honours, declarer did not even have to guess right.

'1440?' queried the North player.

'Yes,' Groetheim replied. 'I was hoping you would re-open with a double, but that's not so good. We would only score 1400.'

4
Imaginative Throw-ins

$\mathcal{A}$ throw-in is not the easiest of plays to perform because you usually have to read how the cards lie. In this chapter we will look at some rather surprising throw-ins. On many of the hands a throw-in would not seem at all likely at first glance.

Geir partnered Lasse Aaseng in the 1996 Norwegian Pairs championship and our first deal comes from that event.

```
North-South Game        ♠ A K Q 7
Dealer South            ♡ 8 6 3 2
                        ◇ Q 6
                        ♣ J 8 3
    ♠ J 10 8 6 3                        ♠ 2
    ♡ A 10              N               ♡ J 9 7 4
    ◇ A 9 7 5 3 2    W     E            ◇ J 4
    ♣ —                 S               ♣ K 10 9 7 5 2
                        ♠ 9 5 4
                        ♡ K Q 5
                        ◇ K 10 8
                        ♣ A Q 6 4
```

West	North	East	South
	Aaseng		**Helgemo**
-	-	-	1♣
2◇ (1)	double	pass	2NT
pass	3NT	all pass	

(1) Weak jump overcall.

Suppose you decide to lead a spade from the West hand. Which card would you choose? The standard 'book' lead is the jack but many players nowadays favour a low card when defending a notrump contract. You need partner to hold an honour, or the nine, anyway. Leading the jack may promote declarer's holding when partner has to unblock a doubleton honour.

On this hand the lead of the jack would have given Geir four spade tricks. West in fact chose to lead ♠3 and dummy's ace won the trick. A heart to the queen lost to West's ace and he continued with ♠J, won in the dummy. Needing at least one trick from the diamond suit, Geir next led ◊Q to West's ace. He persisted with ♠10, knocking out dummy's last stopper and setting up his last two spades. A club to the queen won the next trick, West discarding a diamond. When the king of hearts dropped the 10 from West, the count was complete. West held five spades and must hold six diamonds to justify his overcall. His shape was therefore 5-2-6-0.

The scene was set for a throw-in on East, which would allow declarer to escape for only one down. When Geir cashed ◊K, to remove East's only safe exit card, he was granted a bonus. The jack fell from East! The endplay was now for the contract. These cards remained:

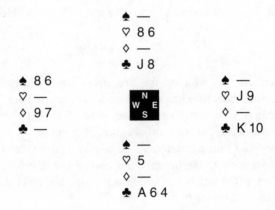

East was thrown in with a heart and had to lead away from the club king at the finish. Nine tricks!

In 1994 Europe played against USA, in a match staged in Italy. Geir and Tor Helness faced Zia and Larry Cohen on this deal:

North-South Game
Dealer East

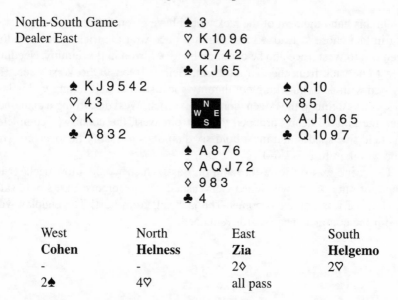

♠ 3
♡ K 10 9 6
◊ Q 7 4 2
♣ K J 6 5

♠ K J 9 5 4 2
♡ 4 3
◊ K
♣ A 8 3 2

♠ Q 10
♡ 8 5
◊ A J 10 6 5
♣ Q 10 9 7

♠ A 8 7 6
♡ A Q J 7 2
◊ 9 8 3
♣ 4

West	North	East	South
Cohen	**Helness**	**Zia**	**Helgemo**
-	-	2◊	2♡
2♠	4♡	all pass	

Larry Cohen led ◊K, winning the first trick. Since Zia had not bid 4♠, Cohen could guess that declarer had several spades to ruff. At Trick 2 he therefore switched to a trump, won in the South hand. When Geir led a club, West rose with the ace of clubs and played another round of trumps.

So far, it seemed that the defence was ahead in the race. Geir won the second round of trumps in the dummy and cashed the club king, throwing a diamond. He then ruffed a club, cashed the ace of spades, and ruffed a spade in dummy. These cards remained:

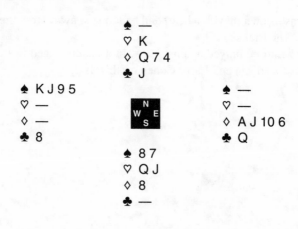

♠ —
♡ K
◊ Q 7 4
♣ J

♠ K J 9 5
♡ —
◊ —
♣ 8

♠ —
♡ —
◊ A J 10 6
♣ Q

♠ 8 7
♡ Q J
◊ 8
♣ —

Geir called for the jack of clubs. When the queen appeared from Zia, he discarded the last diamond from his hand. Whether Zia played the diamond ace or a lower diamond next, Geir would have a discard for one of his spades. The other spade could be ruffed in the dummy.

If Zia's last club had been the eight, Geir would have ruffed the club trick and endplayed him with a diamond.

Norway met the Netherlands in the final of the 1993 Bermuda Bowl. Tor Helness reached 3NT on this deal:

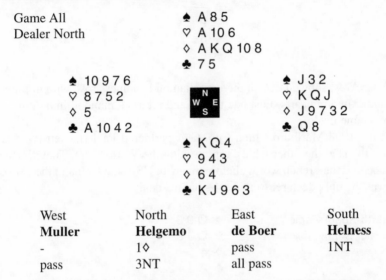

Game All
Dealer North

```
                ♠ A 8 5
                ♥ A 10 6
                ◊ A K Q 10 8
                ♣ 7 5
♠ 10 9 7 6                      ♠ J 3 2
♥ 8 7 5 2          N           ♥ K Q J
◊ 5             W     E         ◊ J 9 7 3 2
♣ A 10 4 2         S           ♣ Q 8
                ♠ K Q 4
                ♥ 9 4 3
                ◊ 6 4
                ♣ K J 9 6 3
```

West	North	East	South
Muller	**Helgemo**	**de Boer**	**Helness**
-	1◊	pass	1NT
pass	3NT	all pass	

The Dutch West led ♣9 and Helness won with the ace, East showing three spades. What would you have done next, as declarer?

Both the Bermuda Bowl declarers (Helness here, Westra at the other table) played a club to the king. Their intention was to steal a club trick, then turn to the diamond suit. As the cards lie, a club to the jack – or even to the 9 – would have been more successful.

When Muller won with the club ace, a heart switch would have defeated the contract. No, he persisted with spades and Helness won with the queen. A diamond to the ace was followed by a club to East's queen. Helness ducked the ♥K switch and won a second round of hearts.

East apparently held five black-suit cards to his partner's eight. Since this made it quite likely that he held the guarded ◊J, Helness wanted to retain a heart as a throw-in card. He crossed to his hand with the last spade honour and cashed the jack of clubs, leaving these cards still to be played:

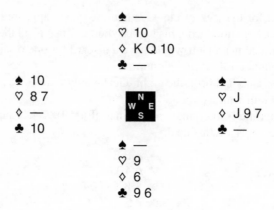

♠ —
♡ 10
◇ K Q 10
♣ —

♠ 10   ♠ —
♡ 8 7   ♡ J
◇ —   ◇ J 9 7
♣ 10   ♣ —

♠ —
♡ 9
◇ 6
♣ 9 6

When West showed out on the next diamond, Helness rose with dummy's king and exited in hearts. East had to win and return a diamond into dummy's tenace. Game made.

In the 1998 Marlboro China Cup, Geir partnered Paul Hackett (with the Hackett twins at the other table), representing the World Stars. They finished 3 VPs behind the French world champions, with USA and China in their wake. Geir was the only declarer to make 4♠ on this deal:

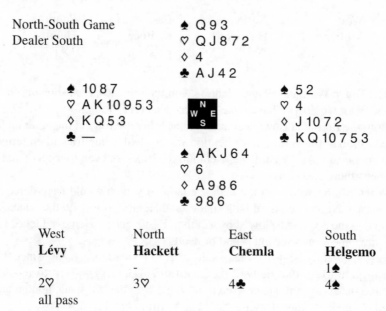

North-South Game
Dealer South

♠ Q 9 3
♡ Q J 8 7 2
◇ 4
♣ A J 4 2

♠ 1 0 8 7   ♠ 5 2
♡ A K 10 9 5 3   ♡ 4
◇ K Q 5 3   ◇ J 10 7 2
♣ —   ♣ K Q 10 7 5 3

♠ A K J 6 4
♡ 6
◇ A 9 8 6
♣ 9 8 6

West	North	East	South
Lévy	**Hackett**	**Chemla**	**Helgemo**
-	-	-	1♠
2♡	3♡	4♣	4♠
all pass			

Alain Lévy cashed one top heart, then switched to a trump. Geir's target now was to score five trump tricks in hand, two ruffs in the dummy, two minor-suit aces, and one heart trick. Careful timing was required. How would you have played the contract?

Geir won the trump switch in dummy, crossed to the ace of diamonds, and ruffed a diamond. He then returned to his hand with a heart ruff and ruffed a second diamond. A heart ruff to hand was followed by two more rounds of trumps, leaving no more trumps in play. These cards remained:

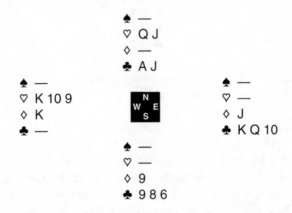

The bidding, and the play so far, had given Geir an accurate count on the hand. He now exited with a diamond. If East won the trick, he would have to return a high club to the ace. West would then be thrown in with a heart and would have to concede a heart trick to dummy at Trick 13. It was West who won the diamond trick, in fact, but the outcome was just the same. He had to surrender a heart trick to dummy and the game was made.

The alternative play at the end – club to the ace and a heart exit – would have succeeded as the cards lay. It would have failed if East held the diamond king (or if West had unblocked the diamond king earlier.)

It is a common situation for a throw-in to be proceeded by a squeeze. A defender who holds several winners alongside a holding such as K-x is forced to discard a winner or two to keep the king guarded. He is then thrown in to lead away from the king. In Britain the play is known as a 'Strip Squeeze'. Americans call it a 'Strip and Endplay'. Both sexy enough names!

Here is an example of the play, from a 1999 pairs tournament in Sandefjord. Geir's partner was Per Erik Austberg.

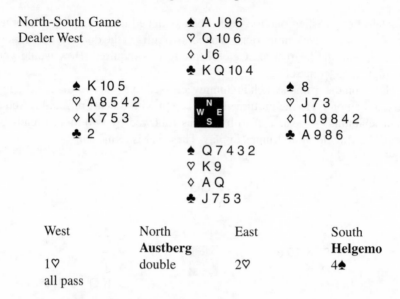

North-South Game
Dealer West

♠ A J 9 6
♡ Q 10 6
◇ J 6
♣ K Q 10 4

♠ K 10 5
♡ A 8 5 4 2
◇ K 7 5 3
♣ 2

♠ 8
♡ J 7 3
◇ 10 9 8 4 2
♣ A 9 8 6

♠ Q 7 4 3 2
♡ K 9
◇ A Q
♣ J 7 5 3

West	North	East	South
	Austberg		**Helgemo**
1♡	double	2♡	4♠
all pass			

West led ♣2, an obvious singleton, and declarer's first task was to deflect the threatened ruff by feigning shortage in the South hand. Geir played dummy's queen, taken by East's ace, and dropped the five from his hand. It was a gallant attempt but East was not fooled. Quite rightly, he reasoned that his partner was unlikely to have led from four clubs to the jack. West ruffed the club return and exited safely with the 10 of trumps. Geir finessed dummy's jack successfully and drew the outstanding trump with the ace. What now?

One possibility was to guess who held ♡J. West held five hearts to his partner's three. One of West's hearts was known to be the ace, so he was a 4-to-3 favourite to hold the jack. Since he had opened the bidding and the heart jack would give him eleven points rather than ten, this further increased the odds that West would hold the card.

Geir saw that there was no need to guess the heart position. An endplay on West would guarantee the contract, whoever held the missing jack. He crossed to his hand with another trump and led ♡9 towards the dummy. West could not go in with the ace without giving declarer two heart tricks and the contract. He played low and dummy's queen won the trick. Geir cashed his remaining clubs and one more trump to leave this position:

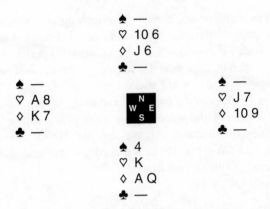

```
              ♠ —
              ♡ 10 6
              ◊ J 6
              ♣ —
♠ —                        ♠ —
♡ A 8        N             ♡ J 7
◊ K 7      W   E           ◊ 10 9
♣ —          S             ♣ —
              ♠ 4
              ♡ K
              ◊ A Q
              ♣ —
```

The last trump put West to an awkward discard. He released ♡8 and was then thrown in with the ace of hearts to lead into declarer's diamond tenace. The bids made by both West and East had given declarer a clear picture of the defenders' distribution. If East had not raised the hearts, for example, declarer would have had to consider the possibility that West's last three cards were ♡AJ ◊K.

On the next deal, from the 1989 European Championships in Turku, Finland, the defenders made it easy for declarer to read the cards. Norway faced the host nation and Sven-Alai Hoyland occupied the South seat.

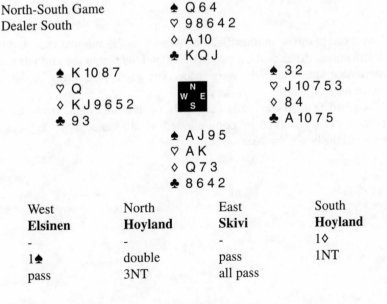

North-South Game
Dealer South

```
              ♠ Q 6 4
              ♡ 9 8 6 4 2
              ◊ A 10
              ♣ K Q J
♠ K 10 8 7                  ♠ 3 2
♡ Q            N            ♡ J 10 7 5 3
◊ K J 9 6 5 2  W   E        ◊ 8 4
♣ 9 3            S          ♣ A 10 7 5
              ♠ A J 9 5
              ♡ A K
              ◊ Q 7 3
              ♣ 8 6 4 2
```

West	North	East	South
Elsinen	**Hoyland**	**Skivi**	**Hoyland**
-	-	-	1◊
1♠	double	pass	1NT
pass	3NT	all pass	

West led a low diamond and Hoyland overtook dummy's 10 with the queen to lead a spade towards dummy. West could see that there was no future in rising with the spade king to clear the diamond suit (his partner would have no diamond to play when he took ♣A). He played low on the first round of spades and dummy's spade queen won the trick.

With two spade tricks in the bag, Hoyland now played on clubs. East took his ace on the first round and switched to a spade, West winning South's nine with the 10. When the diamond suit was cleared, Hoyland tested the clubs, finding that they did not break. He then played his two heart winners, leading the second of them in this end position:

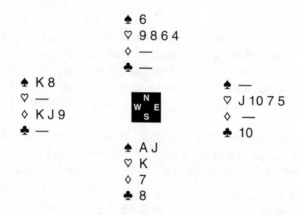

```
                    ♠ 6
                    ♡ 9 8 6 4
                    ◇ —
                    ♣ —
    ♠ K 8                        ♠ —
    ♡ —              N           ♡ J 10 7 5
    ◇ K J 9        W   E         ◇ —
    ♣ —              S           ♣ 10
                    ♠ A J
                    ♡ K
                    ◇ 7
                    ♣ 8
```

West had to throw another diamond winner on ♡K and was then thrown in with a diamond. After cashing another diamond, he had to lead into declarer's spade tenace and nine tricks were made. The game went down at the other table, so it was 13 IMPs to Norway.

Geir had to read the cards accurately on the next deal, from the 1999 Reisinger. (This is scored by point-a-board. A difference of 10 aggregate or more wins the board for your team.)

North-South Game
Dealer South

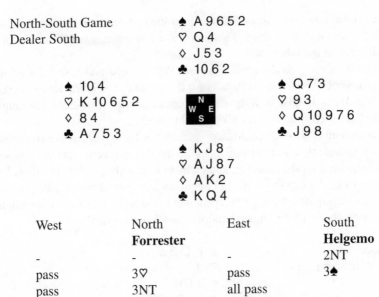

♠ A 9 6 5 2
♡ Q 4
♢ J 5 3
♣ 10 6 2

♠ 10 4
♡ K 10 6 5 2
♢ 8 4
♣ A 7 5 3

♠ Q 7 3
♡ 9 3
♢ Q 10 9 7 6
♣ J 9 8

♠ K J 8
♡ A J 8 7
♢ A K 2
♣ K Q 4

West	North	East	South
	Forrester		**Helgemo**
-	-	-	2NT
pass	3♡	pass	3♠
pass	3NT	all pass	

North's transfer sequence offered a choice of games but there was little to be gained by playing in spades. West led ♡2 (third and fifth leads) and Geir rose with dummy's queen, winning the trick. A spade to the jack won the next trick.

Geir's next move might surprise you. He led the queen of clubs from his hand. West allowed this card to hold, no doubt hoping that his partner would win with the king and play a heart through. Geir now reverted to spades, playing four more rounds of the suit. The ace and king of diamonds were played next, leaving this end position:

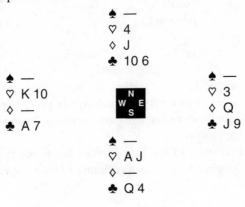

♠ —
♡ 4
♢ J
♣ 10 6

♠ —
♡ K 10
♢ —
♣ A 7

♠ —
♡ 3
♢ Q
♣ J 9

♠ —
♡ A J
♢ —
♣ Q 4

Ace and another heart threw West on lead and he had to surrender an eleventh trick to South's queen of clubs. This was a winning board against the ten tricks made in 3NT at the other table.

How did Geir read the cards so well? West's third-and-fifth ♡2 lead had given him a count on the heart suit. As for the ace of clubs, it was almost certain to be with West. If East held the card he could not afford to duck the king in case declarer then scored two tricks with his K-Q-x.

It may seem that West could have done better by taking his ace of clubs at the first opportunity and returning a club to the 9 and queen. Declarer can strip East's major-suit cards, however, and endplay him with a club to the jack. East will have to lead away from ◊Q and again declarer has eleven tricks.

Geir's teammates in the 1999 repeat win in the Reisinger were Rita Shugart and Andrew Robson. An unusual endplay arose on this deal:

```
Love All                ♠ K Q 3 2
Dealer South            ♡ J
                        ◊ J 8 6
                        ♣ 10 9 8 5 3

        ♠ A J 8 7 4                      ♠ 10 9 6
        ♡ K Q 8 5            N           ♡ 7
        ◊ 10            W        E        ◊ A Q 9 5 3
        ♣ A J 4             S           ♣ K Q 7 2

                        ♠ 5
                        ♡ A 10 9 6 4 3 2
                        ◊ K 7 4 2
                        ♣ 6
```

West	North	East	South
	Shugart		**Robson**
-	-	-	3♡
pass	pass	double	all pass

Some players would have overcalled 3♠ on the West cards. Dangerous, yes, but it would have led to a very playable spade game opposite either the East or the North hand. West preferred to pass, eventually leaving in his partner's protective double for penalties.

West led his singleton ◊10 and East allowed this to run to declarer's king. With no entry to dummy, it would be premature to play a spade at this stage.

Robson preferred a club, won by East's queen. A trump switch went to West's queen and Robson ruffed the ace of clubs return. The ace and ten of trumps put West on lead with the trump king. These cards were still to be played:

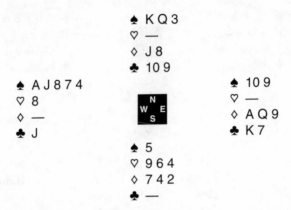

East had discarded his lowest spade, the six, to give his partner a count on the suit. (This could not be from 10-9-6-5 because East would signal with the nine from that holding). Knowing that declarer held one spade, and anxious to avoid a throw-in, West cashed the ace of spades. With this hazard to the proceedings out of the way, he relaxed somewhat and exited with ♣J.

Robson ruffed and paused to reconstruct the hidden hands. West could not hold a second diamond or he would surely have played it, seeking to promote his ♡8. Where was the king of clubs? West had shown up with 14 points already and would hardly have passed 3♡ if he held a 17-count; East was therefore marked with that card. It followed from this reasoning that West would have no safe exit if thrown in with his last trump! The throw-in would surrender a trump trick but it would yield two tricks in return.

Robson duly exited with a low trump to the eight. West had to lead a spade to dummy and away went two of South's diamond losers, limiting the penalty to just 300. Does anything else strike you about the hand? If West had foreseen the throw-in, he could simply have exited with his last trump instead of the club jack.

We move now to the 1997 Bermuda Bowl in Hammamet. Norway were facing Chinese Taipei and Tor Helness was in the hot seat.

North-South Game
Dealer West

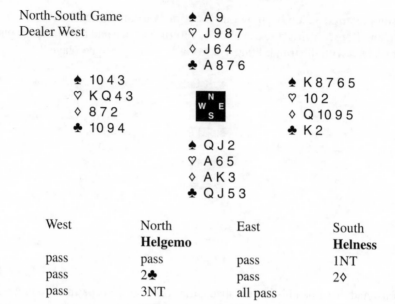

West	North	East	South
	Helgemo		**Helness**
pass	pass	pass	1NT
pass	2♣	pass	2◊
pass	3NT	all pass	

West led ♣10, which ran to East's king. Helness won the spade switch with the queen and led a low heart towards dummy, West rising with the queen. A second spade removed dummy's ace and Helness cashed two club tricks, East throwing a diamond. This position had been reached:

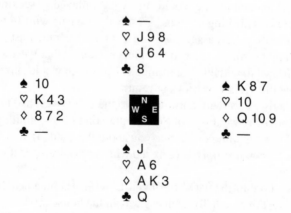

When the club queen was played, East discarded ♠7. How did the cards lie? East had switched to ♠6, playing the five on the next round; it seemed that he held five spades. He had also shown up with two clubs. By throwing one diamond, then releasing a spade winner, East seemed to be holding a diamond guard. In that case his initial shape would be 5-2-4-2.

Helness cashed the ace of hearts, to extract East's last card in that suit, then exited with a spade. East cashed two spade tricks but then had to lead away from the queen of diamonds. Game made.

On the next deal, from the 1996 Volmac tournament in Holland (won by Helgemo and Helness), you may think that a fair amount of imagination was invested in South's bidding!

	♠ A Q 7	
Love All	♡ J 5 4	
Dealer East	◇ J 9 8	
	♣ J 9 7 5	

♠ K 10 5		♠ 8 4 3 2
♡ 10 9 7 6	N	♡ Q 8 3
◇ 10 2	W E	◇ A K Q 5 4
♣ 10 8 3 2	S	♣ 4

	♠ J 9 6
	♡ A K 2
	◇ 7 6 3
	♣ A K Q 6

West	North	East	South
Cohen	**Helness**	**Berkowitz**	**Helgemo**
-	-	1◇	1NT
pass	3NT	all pass	

South's diamond holding did not represent a *certain* stopper, we concede. The Americans were playing the Precision Club system, however, in which a 1◇ opening is frequently made on a short suit. Geir hoped that West would cast his net elsewhere, should the final contract be in notrumps.

Helness raised to 3NT and Geir was over the first hurdle when Larry Cohen led a club instead of a diamond. He won with the queen and cashed the remaining clubs, hoping to put East under pressure.

Declarer would have an answer to any sequence of discards from East. Berkowitz in fact decided to throw three spades. Judging that it was unlikely that East had bared the king of spades so brazenly, Geir led ♠J at Trick 5, intending to run the card. West covered with the king and the eight fell from

East. He then returned to hand with a heart and finessed dummy's ♣7. The second and third rounds of spades drew two diamond discards from East.

Confident that East would not have opened 1◊ on a hand such as ♠8432 ♡3 ◊AKQ10542 ♣4 (and then, for good measure, thrown the four and the five of diamonds), Geir went for the overtrick by exiting with a diamond. Berkowitz cashed three winners in the suit but then had to lead away from the queen of hearts. Ten tricks made.

The most familiar type of throw-in is the ruff-and-discard elimination. You remove one or more suits from the scene, then throw a defender on lead, forcing him to open a remaining suit (to your advantage) or to concede a ruff-and-discard. Here is such a play, made by Geir in the 1995 Politiken World Pairs:

```
Love All                  ♠ 8 5
Dealer South              ♡ A Q 7 6
                          ◊ A Q 5 4
                          ♣ A J 3
           ♠ J 10 9 7 4 2            ♠ K 6 3
           ♡ J 8 5                   ♡ K 9 2
           ◊ 3           N           ◊ 8 7
           ♣ 9 6 5    W     E        ♣ K Q 10 8 4
                         S
                          ♠ A Q
                          ♡ 10 4 3
                          ◊ K J 10 9 6 2
                          ♣ 7 2
```

West	North	East	South
Stetkaer	**Helness**	**Graversen**	**Helgemo**
-	-	-	1◊
pass	1♡	pass	2◊
pass	3♣	double	3♡
pass	4◊	pass	4♠
pass	5◊	all pass	

West led ♠J, Geir winning with the queen and cashing the ace of spades. Trumps were drawn in two rounds and Geir then led a low club from dummy. East went in with the 10 and returned the king of clubs to dummy's ace. These cards remained:

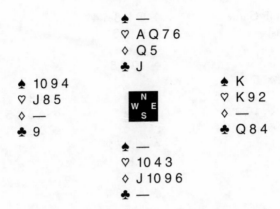

♠ —
♡ A Q 7 6
◇ Q 5
♣ J

♠ 10 9 4
♡ J 8 5
◇ —
♣ 9

♠ K
♡ K 9 2
◇ —
♣ Q 8 4

♠ —
♡ 10 4 3
◇ J 10 9 6
♣ —

Geir led the jack of clubs, discarding a heart from his hand when East won with the queen. East now had to return a heart into the tenace or concede a ruff-and-discard.

As the cards lie, the contract would still have been made if East had found the difficult play of a low card on the first round of clubs, allowing West to win with the nine. If West then played a second club, the original ending would arise. If instead West played a heart, Geir would play low from dummy, giving him a double chance in the heart suit. Here East would have had to play the king to prevent South's 10 from scoring. If instead East produced the jack of hearts, exiting safely in clubs, Geir would cross to his hand and take his second chance in hearts, finessing the queen.

On the next deal, from the 1997 Grand BKS Team Barometer in Ålesund, Geir had to read the lie of the club suit to determine his line of play.

North-South Game
Dealer East

	♠ Q 9 8 6 4	
	♡ K Q 3	
	◊ Q 4	
	♣ 10 7 5	

♠ 5		♠ A 10 3
♡ 10 9 7 5 2	N W E S	♡ J 8 4
◊ 10 9 6		◊ A J 8 5 2
♣ K Q 9 3		♣ J 2

	♠ K J 7 2	
	♡ A 6	
	◊ K 7 3	
	♣ A 8 6 4	

West	North	East	South
	Austberg		**Helgemo**
-	-	pass	1NT
pass	2♡	pass	2♠
pass	2NT	pass	4♠
all pass			

West led ♡10 and it seemed at first glance that declarer was saddled with four losers. Can you see any way to reduce this to three?

Geir won the heart lead with the ace and led ♠K to East's ace. When ♣J was returned, Geir allowed the card to win. He won the club continuation and drew trumps in two more rounds, ending in the dummy.

East's ♣J switch suggested that he held only two clubs. Geir therefore aimed to endplay East with the diamond ace. He led ◊4 from dummy, which East had to duck, and won with the king. He then played two more rounds of hearts, throwing a diamond. This position had been reached:

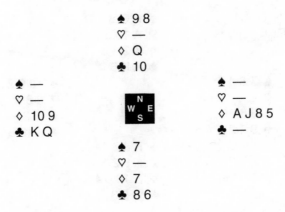

East was thrown in with the queen of diamonds and had to concede a ruff-and-discard. Ten tricks were there.

Suppose, on this hand, that the clubs had been distributed like this:

East would then switch to ♣2, West winning with the queen and returning ♣3. Since an endplay would be possible only on West, declarer would play the Morton's Fork in diamonds the other way round – leading low towards dummy's queen. If all went well, he would throw a diamond on the heart, as before, and endplay West in diamonds to give a ruff-and-discard.

Andrew Robson claims that the next hand is the luckiest he has ever played. It arose in the 1994 Cap Gemini invitation pairs. Tony Forrester had been taken ill and Andrew's substitute partner was Holland's Kees Tammens.

Love All
Dealer East

```
                    ♠ A Q 8
                    ♡ A 10 5
                    ◇ K 9 7 5
                    ♣ A K 6
  ♠ 7 6 4                           ♠ 10 9 3 2
  ♡ Q J 7 4          N             ♡ 9 8 3
  ◇ J 6 3        W       E         ◇ Q 2
  ♣ 9 4 2            S             ♣ J 10 8 7
                    ♠ K J 5
                    ♡ K 6 2
                    ◇ A 10 8 4
                    ♣ Q 5 3
```

West	North	East	South
Westra	**Tammens**	**Leufkens**	**Robson**
-	-	pass	1NT
pass	4NT	pass	6NT
all pass			

Westra led ♠6 against 6NT and dummy, with its matching 3-3-4-3 shape was a dispiriting sight for Robson. Suppose you had been the declarer. Would you have seen any chance at all?

Robson cashed his winners in the black suits and continued with the ace and king of diamonds. He then exited with a third round of diamonds. By great good fortune, Westra won the trick and had only hearts remaining in his hand. When ♡4 appeared on the table, Robson called for dummy's 10. The card held the trick and he claimed the contract.

We will end the chapter with a fine exchange between Geir and one of the world greats – USA's Bobby Wolff. The deal arose in the 1992 Reisinger, played in Orlando, and Geir's partner was Venkatrao Koneru.

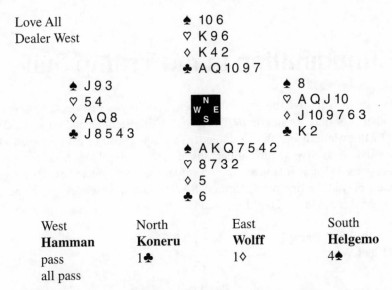

Love All
Dealer West

```
           ♠ 10 6
           ♡ K 9 6
           ◇ K 4 2
           ♣ A Q 10 9 7
♠ J 9 3                      ♠ 8
♡ 5 4          N            ♡ A Q J 10
◇ A Q 8      W   E          ◇ J 10 9 7 6 3
♣ J 8 5 4 3     S           ♣ K 2
           ♠ A K Q 7 5 4 2
           ♡ 8 7 3 2
           ◇ 5
           ♣ 6
```

West	North	East	South
Hamman	**Koneru**	**Wolff**	**Helgemo**
pass	1♣	1◇	4♠
all pass			

Bob Hamman led the ace of diamonds and Wolff played the jack, a McKenney signal asking for a heart switch. West duly switched to ♡5, declarer playing low from the dummy. Already aware of the possible benefit in disguising his hand, Wolff won with the jack rather than the 'normal' 10. Geir, too, disguised his holding – feigning shortage by following with the seven.

As you can see, ace and another heart would sink the contract at this stage. There was no reason for East to place his partner with only two hearts and Wolff switched back to diamonds. Geir won with dummy's king, throwing ♡2 from his hand, and proceeded to run the trump suit.

Wolff could see that the last trump would reduce him to three cards. If he retained ♡A ♣K2, he would surely be thrown in with a heart to lead into dummy's club tenace. He therefore bared the club king on his penultimate discard and followed this with ♡Q on declarer's last trump. His last three cards were now ♡A10 ♣K!

Looking only at the cards East had played, many a declarer would have been fooled. They would have exited with a heart, hoping to force a lead from the club king, and East would then have cashed ♡10 for the setting trick. Geir had paid due attention to West's cards as well, however. Would West have switched to ♡5 from a holding of ♡1054? Surely not. He would have led the 10, giving the defenders three heart tricks when East held A-Q-J-x. Concluding that Wolff had hidden ♡10, Geir played a club to the ace. The bare king fell to the baize and the contract was made.

Hands like that are what bridge is all about.

5

Imagination in the Trump Suit

You are missing five trumps to the queen. Should you finesse – one way or other – or play for the drop? The answer will often depend on a grander view of the whole hand. Which defender can you afford to gain the lead? Is there a risk of an adverse ruff, or perhaps of losing control? In this chapter we will see some examples of top declarers handling the trump suit to best advantage.

Geir played the first hand, facing USA2's Zia and Rosenberg in the play-off for third place in the 2000 Bermuda Bowl.

North-South Game
Dealer West

```
                  ♠ 10 6 5 2
                  ♡ A K
                  ◇ J 5 4
                  ♣ A K 8 3
♠ K 8                               ♠ J 9 3
♡ Q J 10 9 5          N             ♡ 8 7
◇ K 9 7 3          W   E            ◇ A Q 10
♣ 9 2                 S             ♣ J 10 7 6 4
                  ♠ A Q 7 4
                  ♡ 6 4 3 2
                  ◇ 8 6 2
                  ♣ Q 5
```

West	North	East	South
Zia	**Austberg**	**Rosenberg**	**Helgemo**
2♡ (1)	double	pass	2♠
all pass			

(1) Weak two, 5-9 points and five or six hearts.

How would you have played the contract after West leads ♡Q?

The normal first move with such a trump suit is to finesse the queen. That would be foolish here. There is a fair chance that West has six hearts for his Weak Two. If a trump finesse lost, he might give his partner a ruff, then – after three rounds of diamonds – deliver a second ruff. One down!

Visualizing this fate, Geir's led a trump to the ace at Trick 2. He then played on clubs, discarding a diamond on the third round. Zia ruffed with the bare king and played a second heart, East following suit. Geir drew a second round of trumps with the queen, then ruffed both his heart losers. East was welcome to overruff at any stage with the master jack of trumps. The defenders scored just two trumps and two diamonds and an overtrick was made. Switch ♡7 and ◊3 and Geir's play of a trump to the ace would be necessary to make the contract.

On the next deal, from the 1988 Junior European Championship, declarer's problem was to maintain control. Geir sat South, partnered by Tom Johansen.

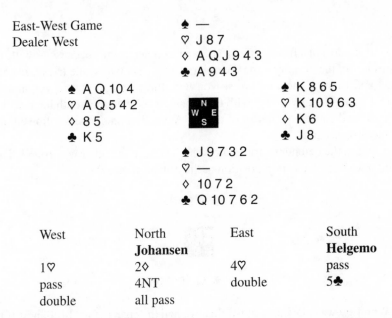

East-West Game
Dealer West

♠ —
♡ J 8 7
◊ A Q J 9 4 3
♣ A 9 4 3

♠ A Q 10 4
♡ A Q 5 4 2
◊ 8 5
♣ K 5

♠ K 8 6 5
♡ K 10 9 6 3
◊ K 6
♣ J 8

♠ J 9 7 3 2
♡ —
◊ 10 7 2
♣ Q 10 7 6 2

West	North	East	South
	Johansen		**Helgemo**
1♡	2◊	4♡	pass
pass	4NT	double	5♣
double	all pass		

Knowing that partner was short in hearts, Johansen contested with 4NT over a heart game that was, in fact, cold. Geir ended in five clubs doubled and the spade ace was led, ruffed in the dummy. How would you have played the hand?

With the trump suit breaking 2-2, it may seem that there are only two losers – a trump and a diamond. Suppose you continue with ace and another trump, though. The defenders can win and force dummy's last trump with another spade. When a subsequent diamond finesse loses, the defenders will be able to cash two spade tricks.

Geir decided to tackle the main side suit first. He ruffed a heart, to reach his hand, then ran ◊10. East won with the king and continued accurately with another spade, weakening the dummy's trumps. Geir ruffed with the four and this was now the position in the trump suit:

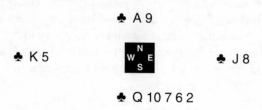

Geir could not afford to play ace and another trump because – with no trumps left in the dummy – the defenders could cash two spade tricks. Instead he led ♣9, running the card. West won with the king and played yet another spade, forcing dummy to ruff with the ace. Geir reached the South hand with a heart ruff and cashed the queen of trumps. When both defenders followed, the contract was secure.

Suppose the defenders' trump honours had been the other way round. This would have been the trump position at the critical moment:

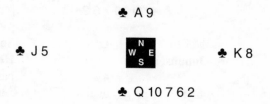

When ♣9 was played, East would have had the chance for a brilliancy. If he played low smoothly, declarer might run the nine to the jack. A third round of spades would then force dummy's ace, promoting the king!

Geir had a substantial side suit on the next deal, too, from the 1999 Cap Gemini World Top Tournament in Holland.

North-South Game
Dealer West

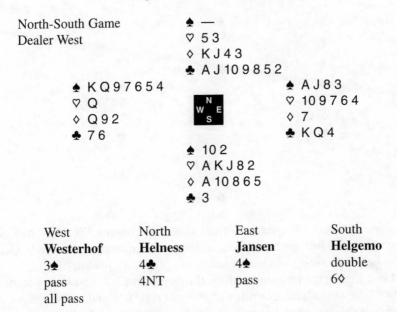

```
                    ♠ —
                    ♡ 5 3
                    ◇ K J 4 3
                    ♣ A J 10 9 8 5 2
♠ K Q 9 7 6 5 4                        ♠ A J 8 3
♡ Q                   N                 ♡ 10 9 7 6 4
◇ Q 9 2           W       E             ◇ 7
♣ 7 6                 S                 ♣ K Q 4
                    ♠ 10 2
                    ♡ A K J 8 2
                    ◇ A 10 8 6 5
                    ♣ 3
```

West	North	East	South
Westerhof	**Helness**	**Jansen**	**Helgemo**
3♠	4♣	4♠	double
pass	4NT	pass	6◇
all pass			

Tor Helness's overcall was based on distribution rather than high-card power and he judged well to remove South's double. (The spade game is one down at best). West led ♠K against six diamonds and Geir ruffed in the dummy. A heart to the ace brought the queen from West and he continued with a club to the ace and a club ruff, both defenders following.

After ruffing his remaining spade, Geir established the club suit by ruffing a third round with the eight. West could see the defenders' fate if he overruffed. Declarer would win the return (ruffing in the South hand if a third round of spades was played), draw trumps with the ace and king, then enjoy dummy's clubs. West therefore declined to overruff, throwing a spade. Geir next played the jack of hearts. If West ruffed this, declarer would discard from dummy and again be in a position to draw trumps. Realising this, West discarded a spade.

Geir ruffed a heart with dummy's jack and cashed the king of trumps, removing East's lone trump. These cards remained:

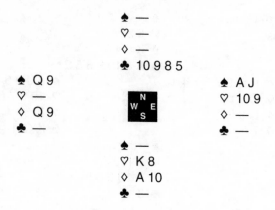

```
              ♠ —
              ♡ —
              ◇ —
              ♣ 10 9 8 5
♠ Q 9                         ♠ A J
♡ —            N              ♡ 10 9
◇ Q 9        W   E            ◇ —
♣ —            S              ♣ —
              ♠ —
              ♡ K 8
              ◇ A 10
              ♣ —
```

Geir now led a master club from dummy, throwing ♡8. West had no alternative but to ruff and force declarer's penultimate trump with a spade. Geir could then draw West's last trump and scored ♡K as his twelfth trick.

Look back at the four-card ending. If trumps were 2-2, East having started with ◇97, he would be able to ruff with the nine now. It would not help declarer to throw his losing heart, because a heart from East would then allow West to ruff with the bare queen of trumps. However, Geir was confident that this was not the position. The bidding marked spades as 7-4 and West had shown out of the remaining two side suits. His shape was therefore known to be 7-1-3-2. Delve under the surface of many apparently brilliant plays and you will find that counting lies at the core.

We look next at the type of hand where declarer's trump holding is not robust enough to draw trumps. The aim, in many cases, will be to score as many trumps as possible, by ruffing in the long trump hand. Geir Olav Tislevoll demonstrated this technique during his win with Geir in the 1996 Israeli Festival pairs championship.

Game all   ♠ 8 6
Dealer South   ♡ A 9 2
                        ◊ J 9 7 5 4
                        ♣ K J 6

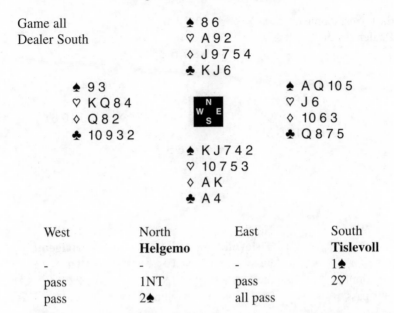

♠ 9 3		♠ A Q 10 5
♡ K Q 8 4		♡ J 6
◊ Q 8 2		◊ 10 6 3
♣ 10 9 3 2		♣ Q 8 7 5

                        ♠ K J 7 4 2
                        ♡ 10 7 5 3
                        ◊ A K
                        ♣ A 4

West	North	East	South
	Helgemo		**Tislevoll**
-	-	-	1♠
pass	1NT	pass	2♡
pass	2♠	all pass	

West led the nine of trumps and Tislevoll won in hand with the jack. He cashed the two diamond winners in his hand and continued with the ace and king of clubs. A club ruff with the two was followed by a heart to the ace and a diamond ruff with the seven. The first eight tricks were his and when he exited with a heart he could not be denied a ninth trick from his ♠K4. Plus 140 was an excellent matchpoint score.

Note that there was no temptation to finesse ♣J. West's ♠9 lead indicated that the trumps were breaking badly and could not be drawn. In that case a club ruff in hand would be just as productive as a successful club finesse would have been.

Geir played a similar hand on this deal from the 1997 European Pairs in the Hague:

East-West Game　　　　　　♠ 10 7
Dealer North　　　　　　　♡ K 9 4
　　　　　　　　　　　　　◇ 9 8 7 5 3
　　　　　　　　　　　　　♣ A 5 2

♠ J 8　　　　　　　　　　　　　　　　♠ K 9 4 2
♡ Q 7 6 3　　　　　　　　　　　　　♡ J 10
◇ 4 2　　　　　　N　　　　　　　　◇ A K J 10 6
♣ K J 10 6 3　　W　E　　　　　　♣ 9 4
　　　　　　　　　　S

　　　　　　　　　　　　　♠ A Q 6 5 3
　　　　　　　　　　　　　♡ A 8 5 2
　　　　　　　　　　　　　◇ Q
　　　　　　　　　　　　　♣ Q 8 7

West	North	East	South
	Tislevoll		**Helgemo**
-	pass	1◇	1♠
double	pass	1NT	2♣
pass	2♠	all pass	

Geir was reluctant to allow East to play in 1NT (the contract can in fact be made on any lead). Since West had indicated hearts with his negative double, the only other suit to bid was clubs! Geir Olav Tislevoll gave preference to spades and there was no further bidding.

West led ◇4, East winning with the king. A club switch (or even a heart switch) would beat the contract now, but East continued with the ace of diamonds. Geir ruffed, crossed to dummy with the king of hearts and finessed the queen of trumps successfully. The ace of trumps dropped the jack from West and Geir continued with the ace of hearts, the jack of that suit falling from East.

A heart went to West's queen and he exited with ♡7. East was disinclined to ruff, with one of his master trumps, and Geir's ♡8 scored. A club to dummy's ace left these cards out:

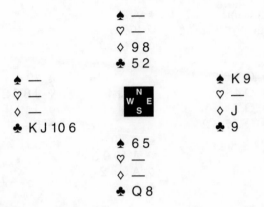

                ♠ —
                ♡ —
                ◊ 9 8
                ♣ 5 2

♠ —   ♠ K 9
♡ —   [N W E S]   ♡ —
◊ —   ◊ J
♣ K J 10 6   ♣ 9

                ♠ 6 5
                ♡ —
                ◊ —
                ♣ Q 8

Geir called for a diamond and was able to score another of his low trumps, making eight tricks and the contract for an excellent Pairs score.

East had a second chance to beat the contract. Did you spot it? He should have ruffed the fourth round of hearts and switched to a club.

(Double-dummy buffs may have noted an remarkable alternative route for declarer. At Trick 6, when Geir cashed the ace of hearts, suppose he leads ♣Q instead! West covers and is allowed to hold the trick. The club continuation is won with the ace and East has to cover ◊9. Declarer ruffs, with his penultimate trump, cashes the ace of hearts, and throws East in with a trump. He will then have to give a diamond trick to dummy.)

Tor Helness had the opportunity for a similar play – scoring a low trump while the defender has to follow – on this deal from the 1993 Bermuda Bowl semi-final between Norway and Brazil:

North-South Game
Dealer South

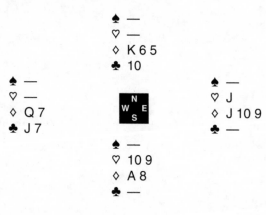

	♠ A 2	
	♡ K 7 3	
	◊ K 6 5 3	
	♣ A 10 5 4	
♠ Q 7 6 5		♠ 10 4 3
♡ Q 4		♡ J 8 6 2
◊ Q 7		◊ J 10 9
♣ Q J 7 6 2		♣ K 9 3
	♠ K J 9 8	
	♡ A 10 9 5	
	◊ A 8 4 2	
	♣ 8	

West	North	East	South
Mello	**Helgemo**	**Chagas**	**Helness**
-	-	-	1◊
pass	2◊	pass	3◊
pass	3NT	pass	5◊
all pass			

The 2◊ response was forcing and the 3◊ rebid a sign-off. Geir's 3NT promised stops in both majors, saying nothing about the clubs. Fearing a weakness in that suit, Tor Helness opted for the diamond game.

Helness won the club queen lead with dummy's ace and ruffed a club. He returned to dummy with the ace of spades, ruffed another club, then cashed the king of spades and ruffed a spade. After scoring the king and ace of hearts, he advanced the jack of spades. West covered and the last heart was thrown from dummy. West was on lead in this end position:

	♠ —	
	♡ —	
	◊ K 6 5	
	♣ 10	
♠ —		♠ —
♡ —		♡ J
◊ Q 7		◊ J 10 9
♣ J 7		♣ —
	♠ —	
	♡ 10 9	
	◊ A 8	
	♣ —	

West chose to play ♣J now. When East ruffed, Helness overruffed with the ace and played king and another trump, bringing down the defenders' last two trumps. Game made.

Suppose instead that West had exited with ◊7 in the four-card ending. Do you see how Helness would still have succeeded? He would win with the king of trumps, cross to the trump ace and score dummy's last small trump by ruffing a heart! Poor East would have to follow suit.

We will look now at a hand or two where declarer has a long trump suit in hand but the suit breaks poorly. French star Alain Lévy was in sparkling form when he played the next hand against Helness/Helgemo in the 1997 Cap Gemini invitational.

North-South Game Dealer East		♠ J 8 5 3 ♡ 4 ◊ A K 8 5 4 3 ♣ A 8	
♠ K Q 7 6 2 ♡ Q 10 9 7 ◊ 10 ♣ 7 5 4		♠ A 10 9 ♡ 8 6 ◊ Q 9 7 ♣ Q J 9 6 2	
	♠ 4 ♡ A K J 5 3 2 ◊ J 6 2 ♣ K 10 3		

West	North	East	South
Helness	**Mari**	**Helgemo**	**Lévy**
-	-	pass	1♡
1♠	2◊	3♠	4♡
all pass			

Five diamonds would have been a more secure game, but this was difficult to find after Geir's bold double raise in spades. The bidding ground to a halt in four hearts and Tor Helness led ♠K, winning the first trick. He switched to a club, won with the ace, and Alain Lévy ruffed a spade in his hand. He had no reason to suspect a bad trump break but nothing was to be lost by scoring the low trumps in his hand.

After cashing the king of clubs, declarer ruffed a club in dummy and ruffed another spade. A diamond to the ace was followed by the jack of spades, ruffed with the eight by East and overruffed with the jack. The ace of trumps drew East's remaining trump, leaving these cards outstanding:

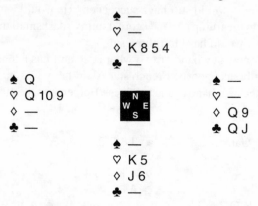

```
              ♠ —
              ♡ —
              ◊ K 8 5 4
              ♣ —
  ♠ Q                        ♠ —
  ♡ Q 10 9      N            ♡ —
  ◊ —         W   E          ◊ Q 9
  ♣ —           S            ♣ Q J
              ♠ —
              ♡ K 5
              ◊ J 6
              ♣ —
```

When a diamond was led towards the dummy, Helness (West) could not prevent declarer from scoring two more tricks for his game. If he ruffed and returned a trump, declarer would force West's last trump with another diamond, setting up ♡5 as the tenth trick.

Did you spot any way to defeat the game? If Geir had overtaken the ♠K lead with the ace and switched to a trump, the game would have gone down. No one is perfect!

Tony Forrester faced a similarly hostile trump break on the next hand, from the 1996 Reisinger semi-finals. His solution was different. He declined to draw any trumps at all!

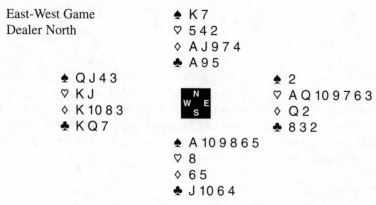

```
East-West Game         ♠ K 7
Dealer North           ♡ 5 4 2
                       ◊ A J 9 7 4
                       ♣ A 9 5
  ♠ Q J 4 3                        ♠ 2
  ♡ K J            N                ♡ A Q 10 9 7 6 3
  ◊ K 10 8 3     W   E             ◊ Q 2
  ♣ K Q 7          S                ♣ 8 3 2
                       ♠ A 10 9 8 6 5
                       ♡ 8
                       ◊ 6 5
                       ♣ J 10 6 4
```

West	North	East	South
Fallenius	**Helgemo**	**Nisland**	**Forrester**
-	1◊	2♡	2♠
pass	3♣	all pass	

East overtook the ♡K with the ace and played another heart, ruffed by South. There was no hurry to tackle trumps and Forrester's next move was a club to the 9. When this held the trick, many players would call for the king of trumps. This would still be premature. Apart from the risk that trumps might break poorly, declarer had his fourth club to worry about.

At Trick 4 Forrester called for a low diamond from dummy. Nilsland defended strongly by rising with the queen and playing a third round of hearts. Forrester ruffed with the five and West overruffed with the jack. The king of clubs dislodged dummy's ace and Forrester still refused to play on trumps directly, cashing dummy's ace of diamonds, then ruffing a diamond. This ending had been reached:

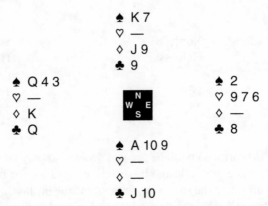

```
                    ♠ K 7
                    ♡ —
                    ◊ J 9
                    ♣ 9
      ♠ Q 4 3                      ♠ 2
      ♡ —          N               ♡ 9 7 6
      ◊ K        W   E             ◊ —
      ♣ Q          S               ♣ 8
                    ♠ A 10 9
                    ♡ —
                    ◊ —
                    ♣ J 10
```

If trumps had started 3-2, declarer could succeed by playing two top trumps at this stage. West had remained silent during the auction, however, despite holding 13 or 15 points. This strongly suggested that he had length and strength in spades.

Forrester exited with his last club and West won with the queen, East following suit. When West exited with ◊K, Forrester ruffed with the nine and led his last club, overruffing West's three of trumps with dummy's seven. The cards lay as he had read them and East could not overruff. Forrester had delayed the drawing of trumps until the latest possible moment! The ace and king of trumps scored the last two tricks and the contract was made.

Bridge With Imagination

Geir made a similar play, when representing the World stars in the 1999 China Cup, played in Shenzhen. He could see that drawing trumps at an early stage would leave him short of tricks. The priority was to develop the long side suit in dummy.

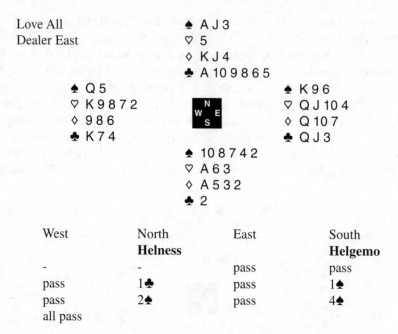

Love All
Dealer East

	♠ A J 3	
	♡ 5	
	◊ K J 4	
	♣ A 10 9 8 6 5	

♠ Q 5		♠ K 9 6
♡ K 9 8 7 2	N W E S	♡ Q J 10 4
◊ 9 8 6		◊ Q 10 7
♣ K 7 4		♣ Q J 3

	♠ 10 8 7 4 2	
	♡ A 6 3	
	◊ A 5 3 2	
	♣ 2	

West	North	East	South
	Helness		**Helgemo**
-	-	pass	pass
pass	1♣	pass	1♠
pass	2♣	pass	4♠
all pass			

Geir won the heart lead with the ace and decided to play on dummy's club suit. A club to the ace was followed by a club ruff and a heart ruff in dummy. A second club ruff set up the suit. Now, without ruffing his last heart in dummy, Geir played a trump to the ace. It remained only to play winning clubs! The defenders could score three trump tricks, but that was all. It may not seem a particularly difficult contract but Geir was the only declarer to make it.

We'll end the chapter with a hand from a 1994 encounter between Norway and the Netherlands, a rematch of the 1993 Bermuda Bowl final.

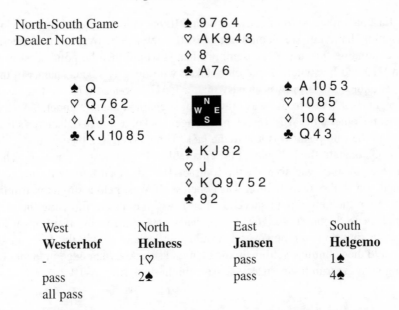

North-South Game
Dealer North

♠ 9764
♡ AK943
◇ 8
♣ A76

♠ Q
♡ Q762
◇ AJ3
♣ KJ1085

♠ A1053
♡ 1085
◇ 1064
♣ Q43

♠ KJ82
♡ J
◇ KQ9752
♣ 92

West	North	East	South
Westerhof	**Helness**	**Jansen**	**Helgemo**
-	1♡	pass	1♠
pass	2♠	pass	4♠
all pass			

West led ♡2 and Geir won with the ace in dummy, continuing with a diamond to the queen and ace. A club switch would give declarer no chance but this was difficult to find. West persevered with another heart and Geir won with dummy's king, throwing his club loser. Geir now led a trump and rose the king!

The trump queen fell from West and Geir cashed the queen of diamonds. A third round of diamonds was ruffed with the nine (it was essential to unblock this card on the present trick or the next) and a trump played to East's ace. This position had been reached:

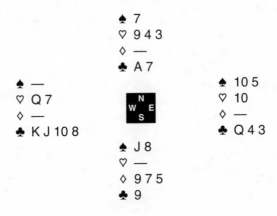

♠ 7
♡ 943
◇ —
♣ A7

♠ —
♡ Q7
◇ —
♣ KJ108

♠ 105
♡ 10
◇ —
♣ Q43

♠ J8
♡ —
◇ 975
♣ 9

East attempted to force declarer with ♡10 but Geir countered by throwing a winning diamond! West could not assist the defence by overtaking in hearts and continuing the suit, since dummy's hearts would then be good. East won with ♡10 and he switched to a club, taken with dummy's ace. Thanks to the earlier unblock of ♠9 it was an easy matter for Geir to lead ♠7 for a finesse of the eight. East's last trump was drawn and he claimed the remainder.

At the other table West found the stronger lead of a club and declarer's first move in the trump suit was low to the jack. Three down was the result.

Look back to the key play at the first table, Geir's trump to the king. This is, in fact, the only way to make the contract. How did Geir find it? If East held a singleton trump, the situation was hopeless. If West held a singleton trump, rising with the king would succeed when it was the queen, finessing the jack would succeed when it was the 10. So, that's a stand-off so far. If trumps were 3-2 with split honours, however, it would suit declarer to win the first round. He could then continue setting up the diamond suit. A further edge in favour of rising with the trump king was that West might duck from A-10-x.

6
Imaginative Play in a 4-3 Fit

When you play in a 4-3 trump fit, the odds favour a 4-2 break against you. It is not always possible to draw trumps. You may have to score what side-suit tricks you can, then score trumps by ruffing in both hands. Geir followed such a plan on the next deal, from the 1999 Blue Ribbon Pairs:

```
North-South Game          ♠ Q J 8 6
Dealer West               ♡ Q J 2
                          ◊ A K 8 6
                          ♣ 9 8
      ♠ A 10 9 7 3                          ♠ K 5 2
      ♡ 8 7 6              N                ♡ 10 9 3
      ◊ 4              W       E            ◊ Q J 9 3
      ♣ J 7 6 4            S                ♣ Q 10 2
                          ♠ 4
                          ♡ A K 5 4
                          ◊ 10 7 5 2
                          ♣ A K 5 3
```

West	North	East	South
	Freeman		**Helgemo**
pass	1◊	pass	1♡
pass	1♠	pass	2♣
pass	2♡	pass	3◊
pass	3♡	pass	4♡
all pass			

It was unusual to settle in a 4-3 fit, when holding such a powerful stopper in the unbid suit. However, Geir could see that it would be possible to ruff clubs in the dummy, while scoring his own small trumps by ruffing spades.

West led his singleton diamond, won with dummy's ace. When the queen of spades was led to the next trick, East played low. West won with the ace and continued with ♠10, ruffed in the South hand. Geir led a diamond towards dummy and West could see no benefit in ruffing. He discarded a spade instead and dummy's ◊K won the trick. A second spade ruff brought down East's king

67

and was followed by two top clubs and a club ruffed with dummy's queen. When the master jack of spades was led from the dummy East ruffed with the 10 and Geir overruffed with the ace. A club ruff with the jack was declarer's ninth trick and his king of trumps brought the total to ten. With most declarers scoring eight or nine tricks in 3NT, this was a near top.

It may seem that the defence will fare better if East wins ♠Q with the king and switches to a trump. If declarer subsequently leads a diamond towards the dummy, West can ruff in and play a second trump – beating the contract. However, declarer has a counter. Instead of leading a second round of diamonds, he can ruff one club in dummy and draw trumps himself. This ending would result:

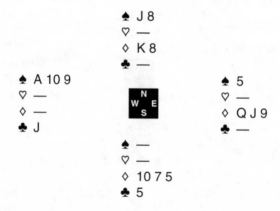

```
                 ♠ J 8
                 ♡ —
                 ◊ K 8
                 ♣ —
  ♠ A 10 9                      ♠ 5
  ♡ —           ┌─────┐         ♡ —
  ◊ —           │  N  │         ◊ Q J 9
  ♣ J           │W   E│         ♣ —
                │  S  │
                └─────┘
                 ♠ —
                 ♡ —
                 ◊ 10 7 5
                 ♣ 5
```

Declarer exits with his last club, throwing ◊8, and West has to surrender a spade trick to the dummy. +620!

Changing the subject, do you and your partner ever attempt the Bidding Challenge hands, presented by various bridge magazines? Every few months they include a deal where the obvious bidding is 1NT-3NT, but both hands have a low doubleton in the same suit and the defenders can cash five tricks there.

When Geir and Tony Forrester played together in the 1999 Reisinger, they had a gadget to deal with this situation. A 2NT response to 1NT showed a hand with an unspecified weak doubleton. If the opener was so inclined, he could ask which doubleton his partner held. It was not long before the convention was put to good use.

Imaginative Play in a 4-3 Fit

East-West Game
Dealer West

	North	
	♠ K 10 9 6 ♡ A K 5 ◊ A 10 7 2 ♣ Q 10	
♠ Q 8 7 2 ♡ 2 ◊ Q J 3 ♣ A 9 7 5 3	N / W E / S	♠ 5 3 ♡ J 9 8 4 3 ◊ 8 5 ♣ K 8 4 2
	♠ A J 4 ♡ Q 10 7 6 ◊ K 9 6 4 ♣ J 6	

West	North	East	South
	Forrester		**Helgemo**
pass	1NT	pass	2NT (1)
pass	3♣ (2)	pass	3♠ (3)
pass	4♣ (4)	pass	4♡
pass	4♠	all pass	

(1) I have a weak doubleton somewhere.
(2) Where?
(3) In clubs.
(4) 3NT is no good, then; suggest something else.

Aware that the opponents were weak in clubs, West led ♣3 to East's king. Let's consider the defence first. What would your next move have been in the East seat?

It is surely right to take the other club trick immediately, preventing any risk of an endplay later. East switched to a low heart instead, however, and West played ♡2 on Geir's ♡6. The fact that West could not beat ♡6 was a vital clue to the play of the trump suit. If East was longer than West in hearts, West was more likely to hold the trump length.

Geir overtook his ♡6 with dummy's ace and played a trump to the ace. He ran ♠J successfully, played a trump to the 10, and drew West's last trump. West showed out when the king of hearts was played and Geir took the marked finesse of ♡10. These cards remained:

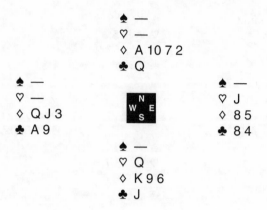

```
        ♠ —
        ♡ —
        ◊ A 10 7 2
        ♣ Q

♠ —                         ♠ —
♡ —              N          ♡ J
◊ Q J 3      W      E       ◊ 8 5
♣ A 9            S          ♣ 8 4

        ♠ —
        ♡ Q
        ◊ K 9 6
        ♣ J
```

When the last heart was played, West had to bare the ace of clubs. He was then thrown in with that card and had to open the diamond suit. It is best to exit with an honour in this situation. West preferred to play ◊3 and this ran to South's nine, giving declarer eleven tricks and a score of +650. The scoring in the Reisinger is point-a-board and the second overtrick was necessary to win the board. At the other table the bidding had been 1NT-3NT, making ten tricks on a heart lead (declarer guessed the spades correctly when hearts proved to be 5-1).

Think back to East's return at Trick 2 against 4♠. Had he played a more sensible club to the ace he would not only have prevented the endplay, he would have left declarer with an even guess in trumps.

A glutton for punishment, Geir played a slam in a 4-3 fit on the next deal, from the 1998 Macallan Invitation Pairs:

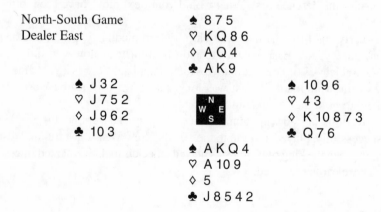

```
North-South Game        ♠ 8 7 5
Dealer East             ♡ K Q 8 6
                        ◊ A Q 4
                        ♣ A K 9

♠ J 3 2                                  ♠ 10 9 6
♡ J 7 5 2               N                ♡ 4 3
◊ J 9 6 2          W         E           ◊ K 10 8 7 3
♣ 10 3                 S                 ♣ Q 7 6

                        ♠ A K Q 4
                        ♡ A 10 9
                        ◊ 5
                        ♣ J 8 5 4 2
```

West	North	East	South
Justin	**Tor**	**Jason**	**Geir**
Hackett	**Helness**	**Hackett**	**Helgemo**
-	-	2◇ (1)	double
4◇	4NT	pass	5♡
pass	6♡	all pass	

(1) Weak two, often a five-card suit when non-vulnerable.

The Hackett twins put up a substantial barrage on their limited values. Indeed, a penalty of 1400 was up for grabs (provided the defenders do not play on trumps, North's ◇Q cannot be caught). A double by Helness would have been for take-out, however, and he opted for Blackwood instead. Six clubs would be a good contract, since declarer can draw two rounds of trumps and ruff the fourth spade in dummy if necessary. Six notrumps by North would also be a fair spot. The opponents had made life difficult, though, and Geir eventually had to play six hearts from the short trump hand.

West led a diamond, won with dummy's ace. Geir ruffed a diamond, returned to the club ace, and ruffed ◇Q. After playing the bare ace of trumps, Geir returned to dummy with the club king and drew two more rounds of trumps. The suit failed to divide, leaving West with a trump trick and East with an apparent club trick. Things are not always what they seem in bridge, however. These cards remained:

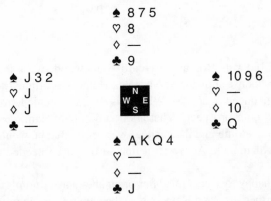

When three rounds of spades were played, West had to follow all the way. A fourth round of the suit allowed Geir to score dummy's ♡8 *en passant*. The two losers had been condensed into one and declarer had his +1430.

71

Our last 4-3 hand comes from the quarter-finals of the 1997 Bermuda Bowl, in Tunisia's Hammamet. This is not a book on bidding but it is worth studying the auction, finely judged by Tor Helness.

```
Game All                    ♠ A 10 9 7 6 5
Dealer West                 ♡ Q
                            ◊ K Q 3
                            ♣ 10 9 8
    ♠ J 8 4 3                                   ♠ Q
    ♡ 7 6 5 4            N                       ♡ A 10 9 2
    ◊ 9 7 2          W       E                   ◊ 8 6 4
    ♣ J 3                   S                    ♣ Q 6 5 4 2
                            ♠ K 2
                            ♡ K J 8 3
                            ◊ A J 10 5
                            ♣ A K 7
```

West	North	East	South
Bocchi	**Helgemo**	**Duboin**	**Helness**
pass	1♠	pass	2◊
pass	2♠	pass	3♣
pass	3◊	pass	3♠
pass	4♣	pass	4NT
pass	5◊	pass	5♡
pass	5♠	pass	6◊
all pass			

The 4NT bid was Roman Key-card Blackwood, with spades agreed as trumps. The response showing one ace and Helness continued with 5♡, asking if Geir held the queen of spades. When this card was denied, a spade slam was known to be a poor prospect. What about a diamond slam, on a 4-3 fit? Geir had opened the bidding and the chances were good that he would hold the king and queen of diamonds. At worst, a finesse might be needed to bring in the trump suit.

Geir was happy to accept this offer of an alternative trump suit. Bocchi led a heart to his partner's ace and Helness won the club return. He ruffed a heart, then led a second club to the king. A third round of hearts allowed a club to be thrown from dummy and a club ruff followed. After cashing the bare king of trumps, Helness returned to his hand with ♠K and drew trumps. That was twelve tricks and 12 IMPs when compared to the spade game made at the other table.

7
Imagining the Hidden Hands

Playing the dummy to maximum effect is possible only if you make every conceivable effort to reconstruct the defenders' hands. The first pieces of evidence may come from the auction; perhaps an opponent opened or overcalled. The next big slice of information comes from the opening lead. This is followed by further clues, every time a defender plays a card. By the time you are halfway through a hand, you will usually have a good picture of the way the cards lie.

The first hand was played by Jon Egil Furunes, in the semi-final of the 2000 Bermuda Bowl, against Brazil.

```
Love All              ♠ K 5 3
Dealer East           ♡ A Q 7 6
                      ◇ 9 4
                      ♣ 9 8 4 3
         ♠ A Q 9                    ♠ J 10 7 2
         ♡ 4 2           N          ♡ J 9 5 3
         ◇ K Q 7 6 5 3 2  W   E     ◇ A 8
         ♣ 6              S         ♣ 10 5 2
                      ♠ 8 6 4
                      ♡ K 10 8
                      ◇ J 10
                      ♣ A K Q J 7
```

West	North	East	South
Chagas	**Helness**	**Branco**	**Furunes**
-	-	pass	1NT
3◇	double	pass	4♣
all pass			

The opening bid showed 15-17 points and North's double was for take-out (much more useful than playing penalty doubles). With the previous chapter in mind, you may think that the 4-3 heart fit offers some prospect of game. The defenders can prevent a trump finesse by playing three rounds of diamonds, however. Even if West leads his singleton club, declarer cannot get home. At the table Furunes bid a straightforward 4♣ and there was no further bidding.

Chagas led the king of diamonds and Branco overtook with the ace, returning a diamond to the queen. Chagas now switched to a trump. How would you have played the hand?

Furunes won the trump switch and drew a second round of trumps, West showing out. Many declarers would now draw the last trump and take some view or other in the heart suit. Furunes decided to delay the decision in hearts until he knew more about the hand. Since he would need to find the spade ace onside, whether the heart suit produced four tricks or not, he led a spade to the king at Trick 5. West produced the nine and the king won the trick.

How much information did declarer have on West's shape now, would you say? The 3◊ overcall might have been made on a 6-card suit or a 7-card suit. The fact that East chose to overtake the king lead with the ace strongly suggested that West held seven diamonds to his partner's two. How about the spades? When an elimination ending is threatened, a good player does not like to leave himself with a bare ace in a side suit. If Chagas had started with ace doubleton in spades, he might well have played the ace on the first round. (Little could be gained by playing low because declarer – knowing that West held the ace when dummy's king won – would surely duck or finesse to the ace on the next round.) Furunes concluded that West held at least three spades. He had shown up with one trump, so he was likely to hold either two hearts or one heart.

Furunes drew the last trump, crossed to dummy with the ace of hearts, and boldly finessed ♡10. With the heart suit divided 2-4, the odds were 2-to-1 in favour of East holding the missing jack. The finesse duly succeeded and Furunes had his contract. At the other table Geir and his partner sat East-West and defeated 3♡.

Here is another partscore from the round-robin stage of the 2000 Bermuda Bowl. (If you're not impressed by part scores, perhaps you should reconsider. It is the area where the expert declarer has his greatest edge, particular when – as here – the trump fit is less than secure).

Game All   ♠ Q 5
Dealer East   ♡ A Q 10 7
                   ◊ K Q 7
                   ♣ K 10 6 2

♠ K 8		♠ A J 10 9 7 3
♡ 8 6 5 3		♡ J 2
◊ A 10 6 5	N W E S	◊ 4 2
♣ A 7 4		♣ Q J 9

                 ♠ 6 4 2
                 ♡ K 9 4
                 ◊ J 9 8 3
                 ♣ 8 5 3

West	North **Austberg**	East	South **Helgemo**
-	-	2♠	pass
pass	double	pass	3◊
all pass			

West won the first trick with the spade king, then switched to a low club. It was unlikely that East held two aces after his weak-two opening. Also, Geir could not afford East to win the first round of clubs with a doubleton jack or queen, then cross back to West's ace for a ruff. He therefore rose with the king of clubs, winning the trick.

Geir's next move was to play the queen of spades to East's ace. His plan at this stage was to ruff a spade in the short-trump hand. The defenders cashed two club tricks and West then switched to ♡3, drawing the seven, jack and king. Geir paused to consider the lie of the trump suit. East had shown up with nine black-suit cards to his partner's five. The heart position was not exactly clear, but the odds strongly favoured West holding longer trumps than East.

Geir led ◊3 from his hand called for dummy's seven. The finesse succeeded and he continued with the trump king. West was powerless. He won with the ace of trumps and returned a third trump to dummy's queen, East showing out. Knowing that West had started with 2-4-4-3 shape, Geir cashed three more rounds of hearts, discarding his spade loser. The jack of trumps, drawing West's 10, claimed the last trick and Geir had escaped for only one down.

When your contract depends on a key guess in a side suit, it is usually best to leave the decision as late as possible. By gathering information on the other suits, you can greatly improve your chances. It is rare to delay such a decision in the trump suit, but Norway's Arild Rasmussen did just that on a deal played against Chile in the 1993 Bermuda Bowl:

```
North-South Game          ♠ K 9 7
Dealer South              ♡ A 10 4
                          ◊ Q 7 2
                          ♣ 8 6 5 3
     ♠ Q 8 4                              ♠ 2
     ♡ Q 7           N                    ♡ J 9 6 2
     ◊ J 9 6 5    W     E                 ◊ K 10 8 4 3
     ♣ A J 9 4       S                    ♣ K 7 2
                          ♠ A J 10 6 5 3
                          ♡ K 8 5 3
                          ◊ A
                          ♣ Q 10
```

West	North	East	South
Plaut	**Sveindel**	**Kehdy**	**Rasmussen**
-	-	-	1♠
pass	2♠	pass	4♠
all pass			

West led a third-and-fifth ◊6 and Rasmussen won with the ace. There were at least three losers in the side suits, so a correct guess in trumps would be essential. Many declarers embarked on the trump suit immediately, soon learning of their fate. Rasmussen saw that he would need to make plans for the fourth heart anyway. By playing on this suit first, he might learn something that would help him to guess the trumps correctly.

Rasmussen cashed the king and ace of hearts and led a third round of the suit, West throwing a diamond. East won with the heart jack and returned ♣2 to the 10 and jack. West cashed the ace of clubs and played ♣4 to East's king.

Rasmussen ruffed this trick and now had to reconstruct the East and West hands, based the evidence provided by the flurry of cards he had just seen. Let's follow his thought processes. West's ◊6 lead was probably a third-best card from four diamonds. West had shown up with two hearts and had started with three or four clubs. It followed that he would hold at least three trumps.

Since the fourth round of hearts would have to be ruffed in dummy, Rasmussen ran the jack of trumps on the first round. He then ruffed a heart, West pitching his last club, and cashed the bare king of trumps. Declarer returned to his hand with a diamond ruff, drew West's last trump, and claimed the contract. Did that seem like hard work? It was! Good declarer play is mostly hard work, with the occasional flash of inspiration or brilliance. The rewards can be considerable, however. In this case Rasmussen collected 11 IMPs.

When you are seeking a complete count of the hand, you must look at the cards played by both defenders. This will often assist you in unmasking any attempt at deception. Look at this deal, played by Tony Forrester in a 1996 Olympiad encounter with Jordan:

```
          Game All            ♠ K 4
          Dealer North        ♡ K 10 4
                              ◇ A J 10 9 8
                              ♣ 10 6 3

     ♠ Q J 10 9 6 5 3              ♠ 8 7
     ♡ —               N          ♡ 9 8 6 5
     ◇ 3 2          W   E         ◇ Q 5
     ♣ A K J 9         S          ♣ Q 8 5 4 2

                              ♠ A 2
                              ♡ A Q J 7 3 2
                              ◇ K 7 6 4
                              ♣ 7
```

West	North	East	South
Ghanem	**Robson**	**Ghanem**	**Forrester**
-	1◇	pass	2♡
4♠	pass	pass	6◇
double	6♡	all pass	

The Jordanian West doubled six diamonds. This was a Lightner Double, requesting a heart lead. Andrew Robson countered by correcting to six hearts and there was no further bidding.

West led the king of clubs, followed by the ace. Forrester ruffed the second club and drew trumps. All now depended on picking up the diamonds and Forrester set out to obtain a count on the hand. Both defenders followed to two rounds of spades, which – after West's 4♠ overcall – suggested a 7-2 break there. Seeking further information, Forrester ruffed dummy's last club. On this trick West dropped a deceptive jack, hoping to induce a false count. If West had indeed started with a 7-0-3-3 shape, the winning line would be to cash the diamond king, then finesse dummy's jack. Forrester in fact cashed the ace of diamonds first. The queen appeared from East on the second round and the slam was made. How did Forrester guess correctly in diamonds, do you think?

On the very first trick, East had signalled his count in clubs, playing the two to show an odd number of cards. This exposed West's later ♣J as a false card. There are two lessons to be drawn from the hand. The first is that you should watch carefully the spot-cards played early in the hand. It is all too easy to reach Trick 8, then to sit back in your chair, wondering exactly what was played earlier on. The second point is that it is fairly easy for the key defender to play his cards in a deceptive manner, once the middle game is reached. More reliable information may be gained from the earlier cards played by his partner. On this particular hand, East's ♣2 was considerably more reliable than West's ♣J.

On the next deal, from a 1997 Bermuda Bowl quarter-final between Norway and Italy, counting the hand would not have provided the right answer on its own:

```
Game All                      ♠ A Q 10 4
Dealer North                  ♡ J 7 6 2
                              ◇ 7 3
                              ♣ 10 6 2
          ♠ 9 8 7 3 2                         ♠ K
          ♡ Q 8 4            ┌─────┐          ♡ A
          ◇ J 9 5           │ N   │           ◇ Q 10 8 4 2
          ♣ 8 3             │W   E│           ♣ A K J 9 7 5
                           │  S  │
                            └─────┘
                              ♠ J 6 5
                              ♡ K 10 9 5 3
                              ◇ A K 6
                              ♣ Q 4
```

West	North	East	South
Duboin	**Helgemo**	**Bocchi**	**Helness**
-	pass	1♣	1♡
pass	2♡	3◇	pass
pass	3♡	all pass	

You wouldn't have pressed on to 3♡ with Geir's limited values? His action was in accordance with the Law of Total Tricks. When you judge that your side has nine trumps between the hands, you should be willing to go to the nine-trick level.

West led a club and his partner played three rounds of the suit. Helness ruffed the third round with the 10 and West discarded a spade, quite rightly seeing no advantage in overruffing with a natural trump trick. Helness cashed two diamonds and ruffed a diamond. When a trump was led, East won with the ace and played a fourth round of diamonds. Declarer discarded a spade and West ruffed with the trump queen. Now came a spade exit.

Helness had lost four tricks already and could not afford to lose a spade trick. He had a certain count on the hand. West was marked with a 5-3-3-2 shape and (with five spades to his partner's one) might be rated a strong favourite to hold the spade king. Tor Helness thought differently. 'Ace of spades,' he said. The king fell to the table and the contract had been made.

How did Helness read the cards so well? He reasoned that if West held ♠K8732 ♡Q84 ◇J95 ♣83 he would have bid 1♠ on the first round of the auction. His actual pass strongly suggested that he had three points rather than six. With a count of the hand revealing that spades were 5-1, the alternative line of playing to drop the king became very attractive.

Geir and his partner, Geir Olav Tislevoll, attracted the top price in the 1998 TGR Auction Pairs, going for £19,000. USA's Weinstein and Garner won the event, with the two Geirs in sixth place. A thin game was reached on this deal and Geir had to read the cards well to make it.

East-West Game
Dealer North

	♠ A Q 5 2	
	♡ 10 9 2	
	◇ A	
	♣ 10 6 5 4 3	

West		East
♠ J 9 6 3		♠ K 8 7 4
♡ 8 6 4 3		♡ K 7
◇ Q J 6 4		◇ 10 9 3
♣ A		♣ Q J 7 2

♠ 10
♡ A Q J 5
◇ K 8 7 5 2
♣ K 9 8

West	North	East	South
Pietri	**Tislevoll**	**Di Maio**	**Helgemo**
-	1♣	pass	1◇
pass	1♠	pass	3NT
all pass			

An inspired ♠J would have worked well but Franco Pietri's opening thrust was ♠3. At another table the declarer called for dummy's queen and had no chance when East won with the king and persisted with the suit. Even if the queen had won, declarer would still have needed four heart tricks and one trick from the club suit to bring his total to nine.

With few high cards at his disposal, Geir decided to extract some mileage from ♠10. He played low from the dummy and won East's seven with the 10. Even if the heart king was onside, declarer would still need one trick from the club suit. Ideally, you would like to lead clubs twice from the dummy, but it was hardly practical to release ◊A at this stage. Geir tried the effect of playing ♣8 from his hand. He was rewarded by the appearance of the ace on his left and now had nine tricks when the heart finesse succeeded.

Suppose the first round of clubs had been won with the queen or jack, the defenders switching to a diamond. Geir's plan was to play a second club towards the king. He would then hope to lose two tricks in each minor, putting the defenders on lead in diamonds to force an entry to dummy.

On the next deal, from the 2000 European Mixed Pairs championship in Italy's Bellaria, Åse Langeland read the cards accurately by asking herself this question: 'Why did they defend that way?'.

Love All
Dealer North

	♠ K 9 2	
	♡ K 6 5 2	
	◊ 5	
	♣ A K Q 8 6	
♠ J 10 7 6 5		♠ A 3
♡ A	N	♡ J 9 8 4
◊ A Q 9 3 2	W E	◊ K J 7 6
♣ 7 4	S	♣ J 5 2
	♠ Q 8 4	
	♡ Q 10 7 3	
	◊ 10 8 4	
	♣ 10 9 3	

West	North **Helgemo**	East	South **Langeland**
-	1♣	pass	1♡
2♣	3♡	4◊	pass
pass	4♡	double	all pass

West's 2♣ overcall was a Michaels cue-bid, showing a two-suiter in the unbid suits. He led ♦A against four hearts doubled and East followed with the jack, a McKenney signal asking for a spade switch. West switched to ♠J and East won with the ace. A second round of diamonds was ruffed in the dummy and declarer was now faced with the task of reading how the trump suit lay.

West's entry into the auction suggested that he would hold the trump ace. If his shape was 5-2-5-1, he would surely have switched to the singleton club at Trick 2. Then, when he came on lead with the ace of trumps, he could cross to partner's ace of spades for a club ruff. Langeland concluded that West's shape must be 5-1-5-2. She led a trump from dummy and ducked in the South hand!

West won with the bare ace and forced dummy again with a diamond. The king of trumps confirmed the 4-1 trump break. No trump was left in dummy, to finesse against East's jack, but Langeland simply played off dummy's club suit. If East ruffed at any time, she would overruff and draw the last trump. If East declined to ruff, she would throw her two remaining spades and lead a plain card towards her ♡Q10 at Trick 12.

Do you signal your distribution when you're defending? Many pairs do but the downside is that declarer can tune in and, as a result, read the cards better himself. Such was the case on the next deal, from the 2000 Norwegian Premier League.

North-South Game
Dealer West

	♠ K Q 6 2	
	♡ A 8 6	
	♦ A 3	
	♣ K 8 5 4	

♠ —		♠ 10 7 5
♡ Q 4	N W E S	♡ K 9 7 5 3 2
♦ K Q 10 8 7		♦ 6 5 4
♣ Q J 9 6 3 2		♣ A

	♠ A J 9 8 4 3
	♡ J 10
	♦ J 9 2
	♣ 10 7

West	North **Austberg**	East	South **Helgemo**
pass	1NT	2♡	2♠
3NT	pass	pass	double
redouble	4♠	all pass	

West's 3NT would have gone 250 down, if left undoubled. This would have been a 2-IMP loss against five diamonds, doubled and two down, at the other table. When Geir doubled 3NT, West redoubled for take-out. Per Erik Austberg had had enough. Knowing from South's double that there were fair values opposite, he bid game in spades.

West led the queen of hearts, won by dummy's ace. West showed out on the king of trumps, throwing a club. He threw another club on the next round of trumps, then a diamond on the third round. That's all many declarers would have noticed about West's discards. Geir, however, had been watching the pips. West's first club discard was the three, his second the two. There was no reason not to treat these at face value, which gave West a 0-2-5-6 distribution. When Geir led ♣7, West covered with the nine. Geir called for the four from dummy! East's ace appeared and the contract was now secure.

How was Geir able to read East for the singleton ace? The first step, we have already mentioned – he had a count on the hand and knew that East had only one club. There were two clues that the singleton would be the ace. Firstly, East needed some values to account for his 2♡ overcall. Secondly, if West held something like A-Q-x-x-x-x in the club suit he would surely have risen with the ace, fearful of a singleton with declarer.

On now to the 1997 Bermuda Bowl, where Norway faced Denmark in a late round of the qualifying stage. Tor Helness needed to read the distribution of the West defender on this slam deal:

```
North-South Game        ♠ A 9 8 3 2
Dealer South            ♡ A 5
                        ◊ K Q 7
                        ♣ Q 9 3

    ♠ Q J 10 7 4                      ♠ K 6
    ♡ K Q              N              ♡ J 10 8 6 4 2
    ◊ 8 2          W       E          ◊ J 10 6
    ♣ J 6 5 2          S              ♣ 7 4

                        ♠ 5
                        ♡ 9 7 3
                        ◊ A 9 5 4 3
                        ♣ A K 10 8
```

West	North	East	South
Blakset	**Helgemo**	**Christiansen**	**Helness**
-	-	-	1♦
2♠	double	pass	3♣
pass	3♠	double	pass
pass	4♠	pass	4NT
pass	6♦	all pass	

Tor Helness's 4NT bid was not Blackwood; it was a constructive move towards whichever minor-suit slam North had in mind.

The Danish West led ♠Q and Helness won in the dummy. He drew one round of trumps with the king, then ducked a heart. West won with the queen and continued with the king of hearts.

The key moment of the hand had been reached. West had surely started with K-Q doubleton in the heart suit. (If he held K-Q-J he would have led the suit.) Helness needed to ruff his heart loser and had to judge whether he should draw a second round of trumps first, with the queen. If West held three trumps, it would be necessary to leave the trump queen in dummy, to overruff if West ruffed. If West held only two trumps, and his remaining trump was not extracted before declarer took his ruff, he would be able to uppercut. His remaining trump would force dummy's queen, perhaps promoting a trump trick for East. Suppose you had been the declarer. How would you have read the cards?

Helness cast his mind back to West's weak jump overcall of 2♠, which had been made on a 5-card suit. Would such an action be more attractive on 5-2-2-4 shape or 5-2-3-3? It seemed to Helness that the more shapely hand was favourite. Backing his judgement, he cashed the queen of trumps. He then re-entered his hand with a spade ruff and ruffed his last heart without interruption. Yet another spade ruff returned the lead to the South hand and East's last trump was drawn. On this trick West was squeezed, having to find a discard from ♠J ♣J652. He threw a club and Helness claimed the remainder.

Can you guess the Danish contract at the other table? Their South player opened 1♦ and Glenn Groetheim (West) entered with 2♥, a pet convention of his that showed spades. This caused some confusion and three rounds later the auction stopped in 4♦. Ouch!

The next deal arose in the 1998 Blue Ribbon Pairs, where Helgemo and Forrester finished second to Greco and Hampson. (This was one of an amazingly unlucky run of five consecutive second places in major USA pairs events, eventually ended by their win in the Open Pairs in Reno, 1998.)

North-South Game
Dealer South

```
              ♠ J 10 7 4 2
              ♡ J 7 6
              ◊ K 8 3 2
              ♣ 4
  ♠ K 9 8 3                    ♠ Q 6 5
  ♡ A 8 3 2         N          ♡ 9 5 4
  ◊ J 10 9      W     E        ◊ A 6 4
  ♣ A 6            S           ♣ J 10 7 3
              ♠ A
              ♡ K Q 10
              ◊ Q 7 5
              ♣ K Q 9 8 5 2
```

West	North	East	South
	Forrester		**Helgemo**
-	-	-	1♣
double	1♠	pass	2♣
all pass			

West's ◊J ran to the queen and Geir played the king of hearts. West allowed this card to win, noting his partner's count signal of the 4. West allowed the heart queen to win too and captured the third round of hearts. The jack of diamonds won the next trick and East took the third round of diamonds, switching to ♣5. On lead with the spade ace, Geir now had to play the trump suit for only two losers. What clues can you see as to the distribution?

East had shown up with the diamond ace already and his ♠5 switch hinted that he might have a spade honour. He could hardly hold the ace of clubs too or West would not have enough for his take-out double. What shape would West have? With only 12 points or so, he was unlikely to have doubled 1♣ with 3-4-3-3 shape. A much more likely distribution was 4-4-3-2.

Proceeding on this assumption, Geir led ♣2 from his hand. East overtook West's 6 with the 7 and returned ♣6, ruffed by declarer. Geir now played ♣8. The ace duly appeared from West and the contract was made.

The defenders' signals provide a rich source of information, as we have seen on several hands already. Geir took full advantage of them on a deal from the 1992 European Junior pairs championship, where he was partnered by Ulf Nilsson.

Love All
Dealer West

	♠ A K 9 4
	♡ 8 6 4
	◊ K 9 5
	♣ K Q 3

♠ J 10 8 5　　　　　　　　　　♠ 7
♡ A K 10 2　　　　　　　　　　♡ Q 5 3
◊ 10 7 4 3　　　　　　　　　　◊ J 8 2
♣ A　　　　　　　　　　　　　♣ 10 8 6 5 4 2

```
        N
      W   E
        S
```

♠ Q 6 3 2
♡ J 9 7
◊ A Q 6
♣ J 9 7

West	North **Nilsson**	East	South **Helgemo**
1◊	double	2♣	2♠
all pass			

The first point to note is that South's bid of 2♠ was perfectly adequate, despite the 10 points. The two jacks were unlikely to be worth much and the 4-3-3-3 shape was unproductive. A total of 25 points does not always produce game, even with a 4-4 major fit, and this was one of those occasions.

West led the ace of clubs, East playing the five, and switched to ◊4 (playing third-and-fifth leads). Geir won the diamond switch with dummy's king, crossed to the queen of trumps, and led a second trump. When West produced the eight, Geir took a deep finesse of dummy's nine! East showed out and declarer now had nine tricks for a near top.

You can be sure that the defenders held their cards tightly to their chest on the next board. Geir's play had been based entirely on logic, however. East's club bid, combined with his count signal of the five, made it clear that clubs were 1-6. West's third-and-fifth ◊4 switch, combined with East's count signal of the two, showed that diamonds were 4-3. If West held a five-card major he would have opened in that suit rather than on a 4-card diamond suit. It followed that West's shape was 4-4-4-1. Many bridge players go through their careers, scarcely noticing any card lower than a 10. Put in the extra effort, watching the defenders' pips, and you will bring home many an extra contract.

On the next deal, from the 1992 Reisinger in Orlando, Geir used a defender's signal in one suit to foresee a 4-0 break in another suit. His partner in this event was Venkatrao Koneru.

East-West Game
Dealer East

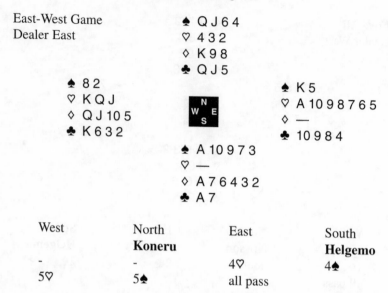

```
                    ♠ Q J 6 4
                    ♡ 4 3 2
                    ◇ K 9 8
                    ♣ Q J 5

♠ 8 2                                ♠ K 5
♡ K Q J              N               ♡ A 10 9 8 7 6 5
◇ Q J 10 5        W     E            ◇ —
♣ K 6 3 2            S               ♣ 10 9 8 4

                    ♠ A 10 9 7 3
                    ♡ —
                    ◇ A 7 6 4 3 2
                    ♣ A 7
```

West	North	East	South
	Koneru		**Helgemo**
-	-	4♡	4♠
5♡	5♠	all pass	

West led ♡K and East signalled with the 10. This was a 'reverse attitude' signal (where a high card discourages a continuation in the suit). If East did not want hearts to be played, which suit did he want? There was only one answer, Geir concluded. He must be void in diamonds and want a switch to that suit!

Geir ruffed the first trick and led a diamond, West putting in the queen. Suppose declarer covers with dummy's king. East will ruff and switch to a club. When West subsequently gains the lead in diamonds, he will be able to cash the club king. One down. Foreseeing this, Geir allowed West's queen of diamonds to win! East discarded a heart and West continued with ◇10. Geir put on dummy's king and East ruffed. The club switch was won by declarer's ace and the ace of trumps dropped East's king. It was now a simple matter to draw the last trump, ruff the diamonds good, and claim the contract.

In the Swiss Teams at the 1997 Spring Nationals, Geir partnered one of the all-time greats, Edgar Kaplan of USA. A sensation piece of card-reading by Geir was reported around the world.

Game All
Dealer West

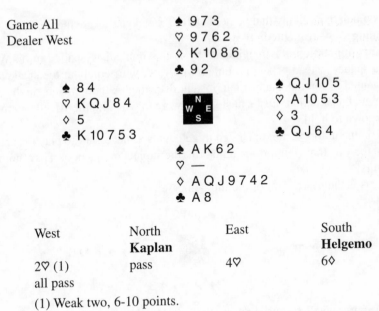

♠ 9 7 3
♡ 9 7 6 2
◊ K 10 8 6
♣ 9 2

♠ 8 4
♡ K Q J 8 4
◊ 5
♣ K 10 7 5 3

♠ Q J 10 5
♡ A 10 5 3
◊ 3
♣ Q J 6 4

♠ A K 6 2
♡ —
◊ A Q J 9 7 4 2
♣ A 8

West	North **Kaplan**	East	South **Helgemo**
2♡ (1)	pass	4♡	6◊
all pass			

(1) Weak two, 6-10 points.

Does the 6◊ bid seem a touch wild to you? It was not intended to be. If North held as little as the spade queen and two or three small trumps opposite, there would be good play for the slam.

A club lead would have proved lethal but West made the normal lead of the heart king. Geir ruffed and drew the outstanding trumps with the ace. Needing three spade tricks for the contract, he now advanced ♠2. West played the four, without thought. Geir called for dummy's seven and East won with the jack. Applying immediate pressure, East returned ♠5. Geir played the six from his hand! West followed impotently with the eight, won with dummy's nine, and the slam was home. Declarer could discard a club on the fourth round of spades, and ruff a club in dummy for the twelfth trick. Had East not returned a spade himself, Geir would have crossed to dummy and run the nine to pin West's eight. The technique is known as an intra-finesse.

How did Geir read the cards so well? The first piece of evidence came when, on the first round of spades, West played low without a flicker. If he held 10-8-4 would he not, at the very least, have *thought* about playing the 10? The next piece of help came when East won the first round of spades with the jack. He was assumed to hold the 10, from West's lack of reaction. In that case, the jack was a false card. Why should East consider a false card if he held J-10-x?

It was much more likely that he held Q-J-10-x and was aware that declarer had a winning view available in the suit.

This impression was heightened by East's immediate spade return. Why play a spade, instead of a club, unless you were worried about the spade suit and wanted to force declarer to an instant decision? Although Geir might still have read the situation, East's best tactics were to win with the 10 – the card he was known to hold.

Commentators at the time rated three talents as necessary to play the spade suit in the way that Geir did: imagination (the subject of this book), psychology and guts!

This is the basic form of the intra-finesse:

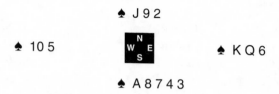

♠ J 9 2

♠ 10 5   ♠ K Q 6

♠ A 8 7 4 3

Declarer needs four tricks from the suit. He plays low to the nine and East wins with one or other honour. There are now two chances of success. If East started with K-Q doubleton, playing the ace next will win. If West started with a doubleton 10, running the jack will win. Which is better, do you think?

Running the jack is better by a factor of 2-to-1. This play gains against two combinations, 10-5 or 10-6 with West, and loses only to one combination, 10-6-5 with West. It is a classic example of Restricted Choice. When West plays the five it is more likely that he was forced to (because he was dealt 10-5) than that he chose the card from 10-6-5. The intra-finesse will give you four spade tricks 6.8% of the time; playing to drop K-Q doubleton with East will succeed only 3.4% of the time.

Disbelievers in Restricted Choice will recite, 'Once West plays the five, it is a 50-50 guess between 10-5 and 10-6-5.' This is a fallacious argument because it takes no account of the fact that from 10-6-5 West might have dropped the six instead of the five.

If you are unconvinced, look at it this way. For every three hundred times that it is possible to collect four spade tricks from this combination, West will hold:

♠ 10 6 5   one hundred times,
♠ 10 6   one hundred times, and
♠ 10 5   one hundred times.

Whether the six or the five appears from West, you will succeed two hundred times out of three hundred by running the jack next. You will succeed only one hundred times by cashing the ace.

The situation is the same here:

♠ A 8 3

♠ K J 4

♠ 10 5

♠ Q 9 7 6 2

If the bidding suggests that West holds the king, you start with a low card to the nine. Suppose that this loses to the West's jack or 10. Running the queen on the next round is twice as good as trying to drop the king. You win against these East holdings: J-5, J-4, 10-5 and 10-4. You lose only to J-5-4 and 10-5-4. Odds of 2-to-1 in your favour, as always.

A rare 'ruffing intra-finesse' was reported by Australia's Tim Bourke:

Love All
Dealer East

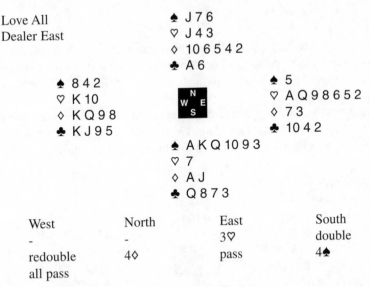

♠ J 7 6
♡ J 4 3
◊ 10 6 5 4 2
♣ A 6

♠ 8 4 2
♡ K 10
◊ K Q 9 8
♣ K J 9 5

♠ 5
♡ A Q 9 8 6 5 2
◊ 7 3
♣ 10 4 2

♠ A K Q 10 9 3
♡ 7
◊ A J
♣ Q 8 7 3

West	North	East	South
-	-	3♡	double
redouble	4◊	pass	4♠
all pass			

West led ♡K and switched to a trump, won in the South hand. Declarer could tell from the bidding that West was likely to hold the club king. He led ♣3, hoping to duck the trick to East, who might well have no trumps left. (South's two remaining clubs could then be ruffed in the dummy.) Sensing what was going to happen, West inserted ♣9 to force dummy's ace. Do you see the 'intra-finesse' position that is building up in clubs?

Declarer continued with ♣6 to his eight, West winning with the jack. A second round of trumps was taken in the South hand, East showing out. Declarer now led the queen of clubs from his hand. West covered with the king and East's 10 was pinned. The trick was ruffed in the dummy and South's ♣7 was now good against West's ♣5. Contract made!

The alternative line was to play West for K-J-9 in the club suit, in which case his king could be ruffed out. However, West held five cards in the majors to his partner's eight. He was therefore likely to be longer in clubs. The line originally chosen was better by about 5-to-2.

The club holding on the previous deal was by no means the minimum needed to set up the intra-finesse. This would have been enough:

♣ A 4

♣ K Q 9 5   ♣ 10 8 7

♣ J 6 3 2

Declarer leads the two and West's nine forces the ace. When the four is covered by the eight, declarer plays the three. West must overtake, to play a second trump, and now the jack will pin East's 10 as before. South's ♣6 is good against West's ♣5.

The Norwegian team of Helgemo/Helness and Aa/Groetheim won the 1996 Schiphol Tournament, in Amsterdam. On the following deal from the event, Geir picked up information from both the bidding and the play.

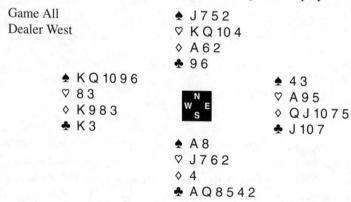

Game All   ♠ J 7 5 2
Dealer West   ♡ K Q 10 4
                  ◊ A 6 2
                  ♣ 9 6

♠ K Q 10 9 6   ♠ 4 3
♡ 8 3   ♡ A 9 5
◊ K 9 8 3   ◊ Q J 10 7 5
♣ K 3   ♣ J 10 7

                  ♠ A 8
                  ♡ J 7 6 2
                  ◊ 4
                  ♣ A Q 8 5 4 2

West	North	East	South
Russyan	**Helness**	**Sobolewska**	**Helgemo**
1♠	pass	1NT	2♣
pass	pass	2◊	2♡
3◊	4♡	pass	pass
double	all pass		

West's final double was poorly judged. His limited defence was devalued further by the 4-card support for partner's long diamonds. Declarer would surely ruff an early round of the suit.

Geir won the ♠K lead with the ace, then made a play that few would consider. He cashed the ace of clubs! A trump went to the king and ace, East switching to the queen of diamonds. Geir won with dummy's ace and played a club, ducking in the South hand. The king appeared from West and that was +790 to North-South.

How did Geir read the cards so well? The bidding made it clear that West held ♣K. East had shown up with ♡A and ◊Q and presumably held ◊J too. Only 12 more points were out, so West would surely hold nearly all of those.

Even when there is no indication from the bidding, cashing the ace first, from this type of holding, has many possible benefits. When the wind is in your direction, a singleton king may fall from West. Once the ace has been cashed, East is more likely to spare you a guess by rising with the king on the second round. When he doesn't, you may place the king with West and try to drop the card. Finally, the fall of the jack or 10 from West may incline you towards playing for K-J or K-10 doubleton, even if East is not the type of player who would always go in with the king.

(On the defence that Geir received, it's true that he would have survived a misguess in clubs. That does not detract from the merit of his play in the club suit.)

8
Imaginative Destruction of Entries

Back in Chapter 3 we saw how declarer could maintain his own entry situation. We look now at the destructive side of communications – how declarer can break the link between the two defenders.

We start at the 1995 Bergen Teams tournament. Boye Brogeland (who won the 1995 world junior pairs with Geir) was in the hot seat. His task was precisely the one we have just mentioned – to cut communications between the two defenders.

```
North-South Game          ♠ K 10
Dealer East               ♡ K J 8 7 4
                          ◇ J 9 6 3
                          ♣ Q 5
     ♠ J 4 2                             ♠ 9
     ♡ 10 5 3          N                 ♡ A Q 6 2
     ◇ 8 7 2        W     E              ◇ A K Q 10 4
     ♣ 10 9 6 4         S               ♣ A 8 2
                          ♠ A Q 8 7 6 5 3
                          ♡ 9
                          ◇ 5
                          ♣ K J 7 3
```

West	North	East	South
Charlsen	**Saelensminde**	**Erichsen**	**Brogeland**
-	-	1◇	4♠
pass	pass	double	all pass

Thomas Charlsen led ◇2 to East's 10 and the diamond ace was continued. Brogeland ruffed and played a club to the queen and ace. After ruffing East's king of diamonds, he cashed the king of clubs and led the losing club from his hand, ruffing with dummy's 10. These cards remained:

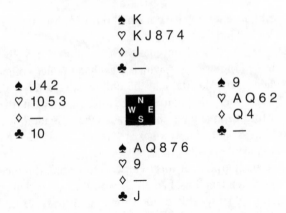

♠ K
♡ K J 8 7 4
◊ J
♣ —

♠ J 4 2   ♠ 9
♡ 10 5 3   ♡ A Q 6 2
◊ —   ◊ Q 4
♣ 10   ♣ —

♠ A Q 8 7 6
♡ 9
◊ —
♣ J

What now? If declarer cashes the king of trumps and plays a heart, East will win and play a diamond to promote his partner's ♠J. Brogeland found the answer. He led ◊J himself, throwing his heart loser. After this loser-on-loser play there was nothing East could do. If he played a fifth round of diamonds, declarer would ruff low in his hand. West was welcome to overruff with the jack because he would be overruffed in turn by dummy's king.

We move now to the 2000 Bermuda Bowl round-robin. This time Brogeland's partner, Erik Saelensminde, is the declarer.

East-West Game
Dealer West

♠ K J 10 8 6
♡ J 10 7 3
◊ Q 7
♣ J 4

♠ 7 3 2   ♠ 9 5 4
♡ A 8 5 4 2   ♡ 9 6
◊ 3   ◊ A K J 6 4 2
♣ K 10 6 5   ♣ 9 2

♠ A Q
♡ K Q
◊ 10 9 8 5
♣ A Q 8 7 3

West	North **Brogeland**	East	South **Saelensminde**
pass	pass	2◊	2NT
pass	3♣	pass	3NT
all pass			

By way of light relief, we have a small problem for you: what would you lead from the West hand?

West's choice was a low heart and Saelensminde won with the queen. He continued with the king of hearts, which West had to duck (otherwise declarer makes five spades, three hearts, and the club ace). Declarer had eight tricks now. A club finesse was unlikely to succeed after East's weak-two opening and he could not afford to give up a club because the defenders would then have five tricks to take. Saelensminde's next move was imaginative – he played a diamond to the queen!

Do you see the purpose of this? He wanted to break the communication between the two defenders. East had no answer. If he cashed his three diamond winners, declarer's ◊10 would be good for a ninth trick. If he switched to a club, after cashing fewer than three diamonds, his remaining diamond winners would be dead. Declarer would simply run the club switch to the jack.

Back to the opening lead problem. There was nothing at all wrong with West's lead but in fact there are two opening leads that beat 3NT. If West starts with a diamond – his partner's suit – East can cash three diamonds and switch to a club. A spade lead beats it too, since West can win the first heart (leaving the hearts blocked) and return a second spade.

The next deal, from the 1999 Lifemaster Pairs in Boston, proved to be a communications struggle between the two sides.

Love All
Dealer West

	North		
	♠ A K		
	♡ A 8 4 2		
	◊ J 9 7		
	♣ A K 9 4		

West		East
♠ J 8		♠ Q 10 9 7 6 3
♡ Q 10 7 3	N W E S	♡ J 6
◊ A K 6 3		◊ 8
♣ Q 7 5		♣ J 10 3 2

	South
	♠ 5 4 2
	♡ K 9 5
	◊ Q 10 5 4 2
	♣ 8 6

West	North	East	South
	Forrester		**Helgemo**
1◊	double	pass	1NT
pass	3NT	all pass	

How would you have played this contract when West leads ♡3?

With West holding only two spades, a double-dummy make is possible via an endplay on West. You run the heart lead to the jack and king and set up a third heart trick. Subsequently, you duck a club and cash your black-suit winners. You can then play on diamonds, certain to score two tricks from the suit since West has only diamonds remaining.

Geir embarked on a different line, which might induce a defensive error even when West held three spades. He won the heart lead with dummy's ace, East playing the six, and led the jack of diamonds. This was West's big moment. To beat the contract he has to disrupt declarer's communications by ducking. (He must then duck the next round of diamonds too, or switch to the queen of hearts to knock out South's king.) No, West won with the diamond king and continued with a low heart. When East produced the jack, Geir allowed this card to win! East had no further heart, with which to dislodge South's king, and had to switch to a black suit. It was now a simple matter for Geir to clear the diamonds, using the heart king as an entry to the long cards.

The most familiar technique for preventing the defenders from enjoying a long suit in notrumps is the hold-up. Would you like to see a hand where Geir held up twice from A-x-x, then made 3NT because the missing ace lay in the safe hand? No, we thought not. Of much more interest are situations where declarer can block the defenders' suit.

Suppose you are in 3NT, with one ace missing that you will need to knock out. The defenders attack in this side suit:

$$\diamond\ 7\ 2$$

$$\diamond\ 10\ 8\ 6\ 5\ 3 \qquad \boxed{\begin{array}{c} \text{N} \\ \text{W}\quad\text{E} \\ \text{S} \end{array}} \qquad \diamond\ K\ Q\ J$$

$$\diamond\ A\ 9\ 4$$

West leads ♢5 to partner's jack and you hold up. When East leads the king on the second round, it is clear that he also holds the queen. Your best play is to win with the ace. The defenders' diamonds are blocked and you will then make the contract, even if it is West who holds the missing ace.

Mind you, a skilled defender would attempt to prevent this by playing the queen on the first trick, continuing with the king. Expecting West to have led from J-x-x-x-x, declarer would then doubtless hold up his ace until the third round.

Geir found a most unusual way to block the defenders' suit on the deal

from a 1997 teams tournament in Trondheim, Norway. He was partnered by
Bjørn Olav Ekren:

East-West Game
Dealer East

```
                    ♠ Q 2
                    ♡ A 7 3 2
                    ◇ K J 10 3
                    ♣ J 8 3
  ♠ 8 7 4                              ♠ A 10 9 3
  ♡ Q J 9 5 4           N             ♡ 10
  ◇ 6 5            W    E             ◇ 9 7 2
  ♣ Q 10 4             S             ♣ A 9 7 6 2
                    ♠ K J 6 5
                    ♡ K 8 6
                    ◇ A Q 8 4
                    ♣ K 5
```

West	North	East	South
	Ekren		**Helgemo**
-	-	pass	1NT
pass	2♣	double	2♠
pass	3NT	all pass	

In response to partner's lead-directing double, West led ♣4. Let's see first
what happened at the other table of the match, after a similar auction. West
again led ♣4 and East covered dummy's three with the six. The contract could
not be made. If declarer won with the king, the defenders would be able to cash
four clubs when East came on lead with the spade ace. If instead declarer refused
to win the first trick, East could play ace and another club and the contract
would be two down.

When Geir played the hand, he calculated that the contract could be made
against best defence only when West had led from ♣Q104. He therefore rose
with dummy's ♣J at Trick 1! East could do nothing. If he won with the ace and
returned a club, West's last club would block the suit. Nor would East fare any
better by ducking. When he came on lead with the spade ace, it would not be
possible to untangle the club suit.

Could West have done better by leading some other card from his club
holding? Leading the queen is no good. South wins with the king and dummy's
J-x will provide a second stopper when East turns up with the spade ace. The
contract can be defeated only if West leads ♣10. East lets this run and declarer
is now doomed, whether he wins with the king or not.

9
Imaginative Squeezes

By way of a crash refresher course on squeeze technique, we will open the chapter with a hand played by the great Tim Seres. Born in Hungary and now a resident of Sydney, he would figure in everyone's list of the world's Top Ten cardplayers.

Competing in the New South Wales pairs, Seres had a choice of squeezes on this deal:

```
North-South Game       ♠ 7 6 5
Dealer North           ♡ Q 2
                       ◊ A K Q 6
                       ♣ A 9 7 6

        ♠ K Q J 4                       ♠ 8 3 2
        ♡ 9 6 4          N              ♡ J 5
        ◊ 10 8 3      W     E           ◊ J 9 5 4
        ♣ J 10 3         S              ♣ K 5 4 2

                       ♠ A 10 9
                       ♡ A K 10 8 7 3
                       ◊ 7 2
                       ♣ Q 8
```

West	North	East	South
-	1NT	pass	3♡
pass	4♣	pass	4♠
pass	5◊	pass	6♡
all pass			

West led ♠K against the heart slam. Looking only at the North-South cards for the moment, how many possible squeezes can you see?

If West has all three missing spade honours and four diamonds, you can squeeze him in spades and diamonds. If he has four diamonds and the club king, you can squeeze him in those suits. What if he has ♠KQJ and ♣K? The single threat in spades will have to be one sitting over him (♠7), so a squeeze would not work unless East cannot beat the seven. (If you knew that West held ♠KQJ and ♣K, you could win the first spade and subsequently endplay him instead.)

How about squeezing East? Yes, you can catch him if he holds four diamonds and the club king.

Enough of the preamble. How would you play the hand?

Tim Seres allowed the spade king to win the first trick. By losing at an early stage the one trick that he could afford to lose, he tightened the end position. This move, known as 'rectifying the count' is a prerequisite for most squeezes. Seres won the spade continuation, crossed to the queen of trumps, and cashed the ace of clubs. This second technical move, known as a 'Vienna Coup', freed the queen of clubs to act as a threat card against both defenders. His preparations completed, Seres ran the trump suit. This end position resulted:

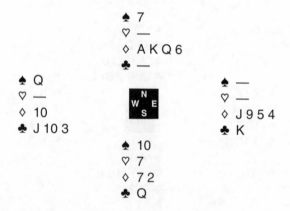

Seres played his last trump (the 'squeeze card'), throwing ♠7 from the dummy. As the cards lay, it was East who was squeezed. He had to release his guard in one of the minor suits.

The squeeze would have worked also if West held four diamonds and the top spades. His last four cards would have been something like ♣Q ◊ J954 and again he would have had no good card to play.

Finally if West held both minor-suit guards, but East had ♣J, West would have been squeezed in the minor suits.

By playing the hand in this way, Seres combined all the squeeze possibilities. The technique is known as 'playing a single squeeze as a double squeeze.'

We mentioned that rectifying the count is necessary for most squeezes. The next deal features a great battle in this area between Andrew Robson and Gabrial Chagas. It arose in the 1990 World Staten Bank tournament.

Love All
Dealer West

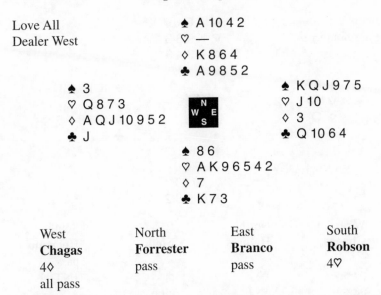

	♠ A 10 4 2	
	♡ —	
	◊ K 8 6 4	
	♣ A 9 8 5 2	

♠ 3   ♠ K Q J 9 7 5
♡ Q 8 7 3   ♡ J 10
◊ A Q J 10 9 5 2   ◊ 3
♣ J   ♣ Q 10 6 4

♠ 8 6
♡ A K 9 6 5 4 2
◊ 7
♣ K 7 3

West	North	East	South
Chagas	**Forrester**	**Branco**	**Robson**
4◊	pass	pass	4♡
all pass			

Chagas led ♣3, won in the dummy. A club to the king, the jack falling from West, was followed by ace, king and another trump. Chagas won with the eight and cashed the trump queen. The defenders had taken two tricks at this stage and Chagas was down to his original diamond holding. Suppose he were to play the ace of diamonds, followed by the queen. Declarer would win with the dummy's king, discarding a club. He would then cross to his hand with a diamond ruff and run the trump suit. When the last trump was led, East would be squeezed in the black suits.

Unwilling to rectify the count, Chagas made the brilliant play of ◊Q rather than cashing the ace. Robson was not to be thwarted. He won with dummy's ◊K and played ◊8, throwing a club from his hand! This loser-on-loser play rectified the count. When he ruffed the diamond return and ran the trumps, East was duly squeezed for a tenth trick.

We will look next at the type of squeeze where declarer does not have to rectify the count. He plans to lose a trick *after* the squeeze has taken place. The squeeze-card forces a defender to discard a winner. He is then thrown in with another winner to lead away from a tenace.

Geir played such a hand when Norway faced Brazil in the semi-finals of the 1993 Bermuda Bowl. Once again, Chagas was West.

99

Game All
Dealer South

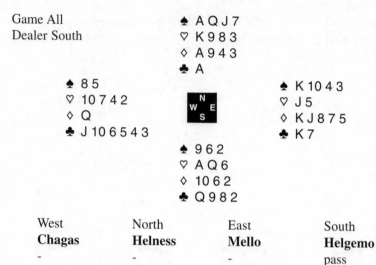

♠ A Q J 7
♡ K 9 8 3
◊ A 9 4 3
♣ A

♠ 8 5
♡ 10 7 4 2
◊ Q
♣ J 10 6 5 4 3

♠ K 10 4 3
♡ J 5
◊ K J 8 7 5
♣ K 7

♠ 9 6 2
♡ A Q 6
◊ 10 6 2
♣ Q 9 8 2

West	North	East	South
Chagas	**Helness**	**Mello**	**Helgemo**
-	-	-	pass
pass	1◊	pass	1NT
pass	3NT	all pass	

With no entries to his hand, Gabrial Chagas saw no future in a club lead. He placed ♡2 on the table. Geir called for the eight and won East's jack with the queen. A spade finesse lost to the king and East returned ♣7, dislodging dummy's ace.

Geir cashed the ace of spades, then led a diamond to the 10 and queen. Chagas gave nothing away with his heart continuation, won with dummy's nine. Geir crossed to the bare ♡A and led a second diamond, rising with the ace when West showed out. These cards remained:

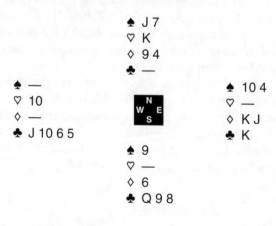

♠ J 7
♡ K
◊ 9 4
♣ —

♠ —
♡ 10
◊ —
♣ J 10 6 5

♠ 10 4
♡ —
◊ K J
♣ K

♠ 9
♡ —
◊ 6
♣ Q 9 8

The king of hearts forced East to part with a winner, in order to retain his spade guard. He discarded a diamond and was subsequently thrown in with a diamond. After cashing the king of clubs, he had to surrender the last two tricks – either to declarer or to the dummy.

Tor Helness played a similar 'squeeze without the count' in partnership with Geir in the 1994 Macallan International Pairs. Their opponents were the eventual winners, Balicki and Zmudzinski of Poland.

```
Love All                    ♠ A 8 3
Dealer South                ♡ 10 8
                            ♢ A 10 8 6 5
                            ♣ 9 6 3

         ♠ 10 9 6                              ♠ 5 4 2
         ♡ A Q J 7 4          N                ♡ 6 5 3 2
         ♢ K J 3 2         W     E             ♢ 9 7 4
         ♣ 2                  S                 ♣ 10 8 7

                            ♠ K Q J 7
                            ♡ K 9
                            ♢ Q
                            ♣ A K Q J 5 4
```

West	North	East	South
Balicki	**Helgemo**	**Zmudzinski**	**Helness**
-	-	-	1♣
1♠	1NT	pass	2♠
pass	4♠	pass	4NT
pass	6♣	all pass	

Geir's best recollection is that West's strange-looking 1♠ overcall showed either spades or hearts. Helness arrived in six clubs, won the spade lead in his hand, and played two rounds of trumps. Had the suit broken 2-2, all would have been easy. He could have thrown a heart from dummy on the fourth spade, then ruffed a heart for the twelfth trick. Trumps split 3-1, however, so some other solution had to be found.

Placing the high cards with West, after his overcall, Helness ran his black-suit winners. This end position resulted:

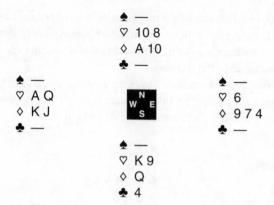

```
              ♠ —
              ♡ 10 8
              ◇ A 10
              ♣ —
  ♠ —                      ♠ —
  ♡ A Q        N           ♡ 6
  ◇ K J     W     E        ◇ 9 7 4
  ♣ —          S           ♣ —
              ♠ —
              ♡ K 9
              ◇ Q
              ♣ 4
```

West had no card to spare on the last trump. If he discarded ♡Q, declarer would throw ◇10 from dummy and duck a heart. He chose instead to discard a diamond but dummy's holding in the suit was then good for two tricks.

Holding all five missing red-suit honours, there was nothing West could do to disguise which cards he was keeping. So, was the contract cold all along? Not quite. West can defeat it by leading ◇K!

Our final example of the 'squeeze without the count' arose in a 1999 pairs tournament in Sandefjord. Geir's partner was Per Erik Austberg.

East-West Game   ♠ K 10 8
Dealer West   ♡ 9 6 4
                          ◇ A J 8 6
                          ♣ A 9 2

```
  ♠ 9 7 6 5 4 2              ♠ A Q J 3
  ♡ 7             N          ♡ J 8 2
  ◇ 7 5 3      W     E       ◇ 9 4 2
  ♣ K 7 4         S          ♣ J 10 5
              ♠ —
              ♡ A K Q 10 5 3
              ◇ K Q 10
              ♣ Q 8 6 3
```

West	North **Austberg**	East	South **Helgemo**
pass	1◇	pass	1♡
pass	1NT	pass	3♡
pass	4♣	pass	6♡
all pass			

West led ♣4 (third and fifth leads) and Geir ruffed East's jack. Trumps were drawn in three rounds and the problem now was to generate a second trick from the club suit. The simple line of leading towards the queen would succeed only when East held the king, or when the jack and 10 fell doubleton. An intra-finesse was possible (low to the eight, then run the queen), but this was well against the odds.

Geir decided to apply some pressure by running red-suit winners before making the first play in clubs. This end position resulted:

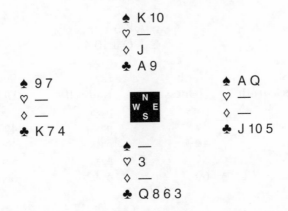

East was in trouble when ◊J was played. If he threw the spade queen, Geir would be able to ruff out the ace, setting up dummy's king as his twelfth trick. East chose instead to throw ♣5, Geir also discarding a club. The ace of clubs dropped East's 10 and the ♣9 was covered by the jack, queen and king. South's ♣8 was now good for the slam-going trick!

On the next deal, from a 1994 match between Europe and USA, Geir and Tor Helness faced the mighty Meckstroth and Rodwell. The battle on this particular hand concerned the entries that declarer would need for the squeeze.

Love All
Dealer North

```
                        ♠ A 8 4
                        ♡ 10 7 4
                        ◊ Q 8 6 4 3
                        ♣ 9 2
    ♠ 9 3                                    ♠ Q J 7 5 2
    ♡ J 9 8 6 2            N                 ♡ Q 5 3
    ◊ J                  W   E               ◊ 10 9 7 2
    ♣ K 8 7 5 3            S                 ♣ 6
                        ♠ K 10 6
                        ♡ A K
                        ◊ A K 5
                        ♣ A Q J 10 4
```

West	North	East	South
Meckstroth	**Helness**	**Rodwell**	**Helgemo**
-	pass	pass	2♣
pass	3◊	pass	4◊
pass	4♠	pass	4NT
pass	5◊	pass	5NT
pass	6◊	pass	6NT
all pass			

Meckstroth led ♡9, won in the South hand. The ace of diamonds dropped the jack from West and Geir continued with a low diamond to the queen, West discarding a heart. Geir ran ♣9 to West's king and the first key moment of the hand had been reached. Suppose you had been West. What would you have returned?

If West had returned a heart or a club, twelve tricks would have been easy. Geir would have cashed his remaining winners in hearts and clubs, squeezing East in the other two suits. A player of Meckstroth's standing had no difficulty in foreseeing this. He found the best return of ♣9, disrupting the entries that would be needed for a simple squeeze in spades and diamonds.

Geir won East's jack of spades with the king and proceeded to cash his winners in hearts and clubs. This, more complicated, end position arose:

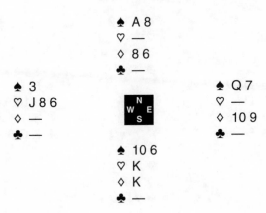

♠ A 8
♡ —
◇ 8 6
♣ —

♠ 3
♡ J 8 6
◇ —
♣ —

♠ Q 7
♡ —
◇ 10 9
♣ —

♠ 10 6
♡ K
◇ K
♣ —

Geir led ♡K and threw ♠8 from dummy. Rodwell, East, had no card to spare. If he threw a diamond, declarer would cash the diamond king and cross to the spade ace to score ◇8. If instead East threw a spade, declarer would cross to the ace of spades and return to the diamond king to score the established ♠10. The position – a rare one – is known as a criss-cross squeeze.

One final point, before we leave the hand. Did you note Geir's choice of 6NT as the final contract? A small slam in diamonds would have had no chance at all. Geir preferred notrumps because twelve tricks might well be possible without bringing in the diamond suit.

On the next deal, from the 1994 Generali World Masters Individual, Geir had to make what transpired to be a critical discard at Trick 1. What would your choice have been?

Love All
Dealer South

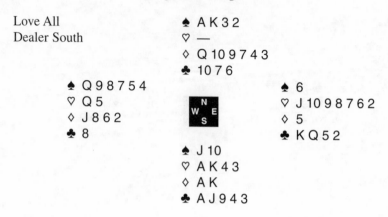

♠ A K 3 2
♡ —
◊ Q 10 9 7 4 3
♣ 10 7 6

♠ Q 9 8 7 5 4
♡ Q 5
◊ J 8 6 2
♣ 8

♠ 6
♡ J 10 9 8 7 6 2
◊ 5
♣ K Q 5 2

♠ J 10
♡ A K 4 3
◊ A K
♣ A J 9 4 3

West	North	East	South
Mouiel	**Chemla**	**Forrester**	**Helgemo**
-	-	-	1♣
2♠	3◊	3♡	3♠
pass	4◊	pass	4♡
double	redouble	pass	5♣
pass	6♣	pass	6NT
all pass			

West led the queen of hearts and Geir could count twelve top tricks if the diamond suit came in (the spade finesse was surely right, on the bidding). He threw a club from dummy and won the trick with the heart ace. When he cashed the two top diamonds, bad news arrived. East showed out on the second round.

The jack of spades was covered by the queen and ace. Geir then led ♣10, also covered by the queen and ace. An ominous eight fell from West. At this stage Geir began to regret his club discard at Trick 1. Why hadn't he thrown a spade, he was asking himself. A low club to dummy's bare seven would clearly be ducked by Forrester in the East seat. Locked in the dummy, declarer would then lose a diamond and a spade. The only remaining chance was that East had started with ♣K-Q-x. Geir therefore exited with the jack of clubs (to retain the lead in the South hand, should East duck). He eventually went two down when West showed out.

Suppose a spade is thrown from dummy at Trick 1. Declarer can then play a club to the seven on the second round of the suit. Whether East wins this trick or the next round of clubs, he will have to return the lead to the South hand. When declarer cashes his club and heart winners, this ending will arise:

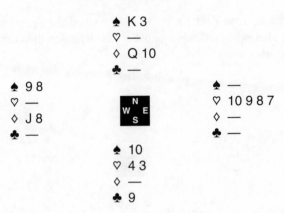

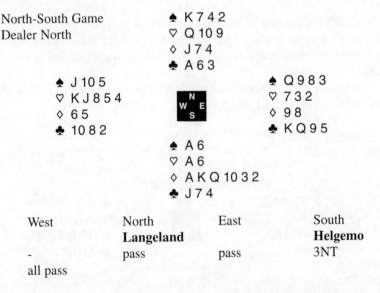

The last club squeezes West for a twelfth trick.

The double squeeze occurs with some regularity. Each defender has to guard a different one-card menace and neither can then guard the menace that is accompanied by an entry. Geir employed the technique on a hand from the 2000 European mixed pairs championship, where he was partnered by Åse Langeland:

West	North	East	South
	Langeland		**Helgemo**
-	pass	pass	3NT
all pass			

West led ♡5, dummy's nine winning the trick. Eleven tricks were on view and Geir now led a low club from dummy. East went in with the club king and exited with a heart to declarer's ace. Geir cashed the ace of clubs, a Vienna Coup to free his ♣J as a threat against either defender, then ran the diamonds. This end position arose:

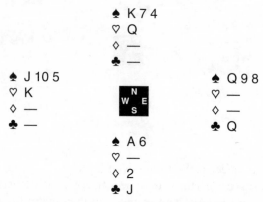

```
              ♠ K 7 4
              ♡ Q
              ◊ —
              ♣ —
♠ J 10 5                      ♠ Q 9 8
♡ K              N           ♡ —
◊ —           W     E        ◊ —
♣ —              S           ♣ Q
              ♠ A 6
              ♡ —
              ◊ 2
              ♣ J
```

It was a classic double squeeze ending. When the last diamond was led, West had to guard the hearts and East had to guard the clubs; neither defender could retain three spades and twelve tricks resulted for an excellent matchpoint score.

It doesn't happen very often, but sometimes a squeeze can yield two tricks. A defender who guards three suits is forced to throw one of his guards. Declarer then cashes the winner that has been established, squeezing the poor victim again.

Geir played such a hand during a 1993 Pairs tournament in Trondheim, Norway. His partner was Lasse Aaseng.

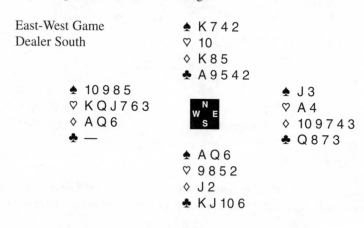

```
East-West Game        ♠ K 7 4 2
Dealer South          ♡ 10
                      ◊ K 8 5
                      ♣ A 9 5 4 2
   ♠ 10 9 8 5                         ♠ J 3
   ♡ K Q J 7 6 3        N            ♡ A 4
   ◊ A Q 6           W     E          ◊ 10 9 7 4 3
   ♣ —                  S             ♣ Q 8 7 3
                      ♠ A Q 6
                      ♡ 9 8 5 2
                      ◊ J 2
                      ♣ K J 10 6
```

108

West	North **Aaseng**	East	South **Helgemo**
-	-	-	1♣
1♡	2♡	double	pass
4♡	5♣	double	all pass

The auction contains two useful calls that you should have in your armoury. North's 2♡ cue-bid shows a sound raise of partner's clubs to the three-level at least. This frees a direct raise of 3♣ to indicate a pre-emptive raise. East's double of the cue-bid is a worthwhile weapon, too. It suggests a doubleton honour in hearts and means 'I can't raise you but I would like a heart lead.'

Geir ended in five clubs doubled and West led the king of hearts. East overtook with the ace and returned another heart, ruffed in the dummy. Since West apparently held six hearts to his partner's two, it was natural to play East for the trump length. Geir ran the nine of trumps successfully, West showing out, and continued with a trump to the 10. A diamond to the king was followed by a spade to the ace, a heart ruff with the ace, and a trump to the jack. These cards remained:

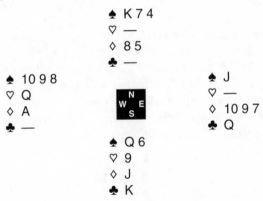

When the king of trumps was played, West threw ◊A in the hope that his partner held ◊J. No, Geir produced this card on the next trick and West was squeezed again. Five clubs doubled had been made with a overtrick. West could have saved a trick by throwing a spade in the end position shown. Since it was clear that minus 550 would not send many matchpoints in his direction, he was surely right to try to beat the contract.

Casting a quick eye over the final deal of the chapter, from the 1996 Israeli Festival in Tel Aviv, you would scarcely think that any squeeze was possible.

North-South Game
Dealer North

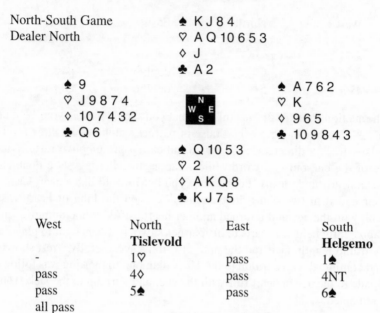

♠ K J 8 4
♥ A Q 10 6 5 3
◇ J
♣ A 2

♠ 9
♥ J 9 8 7 4
◇ 10 7 4 3 2
♣ Q 6

♠ A 7 6 2
♥ K
◇ 9 6 5
♣ 10 9 8 4 3

♠ Q 10 5 3
♥ 2
◇ A K Q 8
♣ K J 7 5

West	North **Tislevold**	East	South **Helgemo**
-	1♥	pass	1♠
pass	4◇	pass	4NT
pass	5♠	pass	6♠
all pass			

Norway (the eventual winners) faced Germany and Geir arrived in 6♠. West led ♣Q, won with the ace. How would you play the slam?

At Trick 2 Geir led ♠J, ducked by East. A trump to the queen won the next trick, West showing out, and Geir played a third trump to the king and ace. Winning the club return with the king. Geir ruffed his club loser and returned to his hand by overtaking ◇J, sacrificing a trick in that suit. When Geir drew the last trump and cashed his minor-suit winners, this ending resulted:

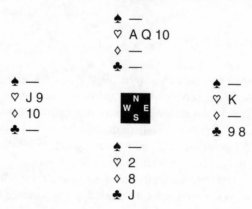

♠ —
♥ A Q 10
◇ —
♣ —

♠ —
♥ J 9
◇ 10
♣ —

♠ —
♥ K
◇ —
♣ 9 8

♠ —
♥ 2
◇ 8
♣ J

West had to throw ♡9 on the last club, to preserve his diamond guard. When Geir led a heart towards dummy's ace-queen at Trick 12, the jack showed from West. What now?

Geir paused to reconstruct the hands. If West's remaining card was ♡K, East would have started with 4-0-4-5 shape. He would surely have made a Lightner Double, requesting a heart lead! On that basis, East had to hold the king of hearts. 'Play the ace,' said Geir. The king fell to the baize and the slam was made. The play is known as a show-up squeeze.

As it happens, another beautiful squeeze ending might have arisen on the very same deal. Suppose declarer wins the club lead with the ace, crosses to the king of clubs and leads a low club. West may try his luck with ♣9, overruffed with dummy's jack. Declarer plays a trump to the queen, then a trump to the king. East ducks the first two rounds of trumps and wins the third round. If East plays a diamond now, declarer must win in his hand, sacrificing the jack, and Geir's original ending will arise. Suppose instead that East locks declarer in the dummy by playing the king of hearts. Declarer calls for the queen of hearts, hoping to throw his loser in the blocked diamond suit. East ruffs, declarer overruffs, and this ending has been reached:

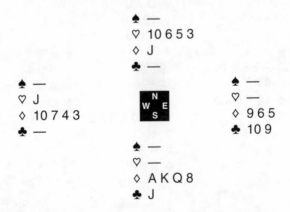

What can West discard on ♣J? If he throws ♡J, declarer will cross to the jack of diamonds and score three heart tricks. If instead he throws a diamond, declarer will score four diamond tricks in his hand.

10
Imaginative Switches

A rather pompous veteran player in Hampshire used to say 'I can forgive partner for making the wrong lead, but I'll never forgive him for missing the right switch.'

Not the most gracious of observations, but there was an element of truth in it. The opening lead is made on limited information – your own cards and the bidding. When the chance for a switch comes, more evidence will have been accumulated.

In this chapter we look at some situations where a key switch was required. We start at the 1995 Norwegian Pairs championship, where Geir was partnered by Lasse Aaseng.

```
Love All                    ♠ K Q 6 4
Dealer South                ♡ Q J 6
                            ◊ 10 8 6
                            ♣ A K 8
        ♠ 9                                   ♠ J 7
        ♡ A 8 5 3 2         ┌─────────┐       ♡ K 9 4
        ◊ 9 4               │   N     │       ◊ A Q J 7 5 2
        ♣ 10 7 5 4 3        │ W   E   │       ♣ Q J
                            │   S     │
                            └─────────┘
                            ♠ A 10 8 5 3 2
                            ♡ 10 7
                            ◊ K 3
                            ♣ 9 6 2
```

West	North	East	South
Aaseng		**Helgemo**	
-	-	-	2◊ (1)
pass	2NT (2)	3◊	3♠
pass	4♠	all pass	

(1) Multi, usually a weak-two in spades or hearts.
(2) Relay.

West led ◊9, won by East's ace. What would most players return now, would you say? They would play back ◊Q, hoping that partner could ruff. It's not a good prospect. West has one spade to South's six and therefore twelve vacant spaces for diamonds to South's seven. The odds are high that West holds two diamonds rather then one.

Geir spotted a more pressing need. To set up a club trick before declarer could establish a discard on dummy's heart suit. He switched to ♣Q and declarer won in the dummy. After drawing one round of trumps with the king, declarer called for dummy's ♡6. This was the second key moment for the defence. Since Geir held only two clubs, it was essential that he won the first heart trick, leaving partner's high heart intact as an entry.

Geir rose with the king of hearts and persisted with ♣J. Declarer had to give up. The defenders scored one club trick to go with their red-suit winners and the game was one down.

When playing pairs, it is essential to grab what tricks you can before the awful moment when declarer faces his cards and says 'the rest are mine'. In 1996 Geir won the Generali World Masters individual championship, a pairs-scoring event. His three table mates were all French past or present world champions when this deal arose:

Game All
Dealer East

```
                  ♠ 9 3 2
                  ♡ A K J 8 2
                  ◊ —
                  ♣ A K J 9 7
   ♠ K Q 6                        ♠ A 10 4
   ♡ 7 6 5         N              ♡ Q 9 3
   ◊ Q J 9 5 3 2  W   E           ◊ 10 6 4
   ♣ 6               S            ♣ 10 8 5 4
                  ♠ J 8 7 5
                  ♡ 10 4
                  ◊ A K 8 7
                  ♣ Q 3 2
```

West	North	East	South
Chemla	**Multon**	**Helgemo**	**Mouiel**
-	-	pass	pass
pass	1♡	pass	1♠
2◊	3♣	pass	3NT
all pass			

Paul Chemla led the queen of diamonds to declarer's king and Hervé Mouiel then led a heart to the jack and queen. Most players would have returned a diamond without giving the matter any thought. Geir had taken note, however, of the ease with which declarer had won the first diamond. If he held the king without the ace, might he not have considered a hold-up? Geir concluded from the manner in which the first trick had been won that the lead had been from a queen-jack holding, rather than one headed by the ace-queen-jack. And, in that case, what points could Chemla hold other than something in spades? Geir switched to a spade and the defenders claimed three tricks in the suit, scoring a joint top for restricting declarer to his contract.

Take the West cards below and see if you can do better than the original defender. Will it make you nervous to hear that the declarer is Tony Forrester?

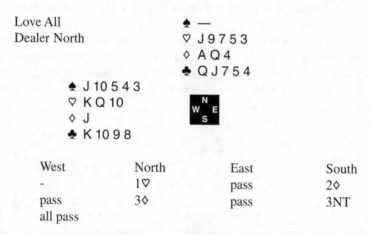

Love All
Dealer North

♠ —
♥ J 9 7 5 3
♦ A Q 4
♣ Q J 7 5 4

♠ J 10 5 4 3
♥ K Q 10
♦ J
♣ K 10 9 8

West	North	East	South
-	1♥	pass	2♦
pass	3♦	pass	3NT
all pass			

You lead ♣4 against 3NT. East wins with the ace and returns ♠9 to South's king. Declarer now leads ♣3 from his hand. How will you defend?

The original West rose with the king and cleared the spade suit. Forrester produced the ace of clubs and proceeded to cash eleven tricks. Meanwhile, a heart switch from West would have put the contract one down. (South held ♠KQ76 ♥42 ♦K10532 ♣A3).

It was a clever psychological play by Forrester to lead a low club from hand, spurning the genuine chance of crossing to a diamond and running the club queen. Even so, West should not have fallen for it. If South held the ace of hearts and not the ace of clubs, he would surely have bid 3♠ instead of 3NT. His chosen 3NT rebid strongly suggested that he held the club ace. In that case

West could count two spades, the club ace, and a likely five diamond tricks for declarer. That was a total of eight. The club queen would bump this to nine. It followed that West's only chance was to rise with the club king and switch to hearts.

In the 1994 Macallan International Pairs, Geir and Tor Helness faced Bob Hamman and Zia Mahmood. Hamman found a great switch on this board, to prevent Geir from making a doubled game:

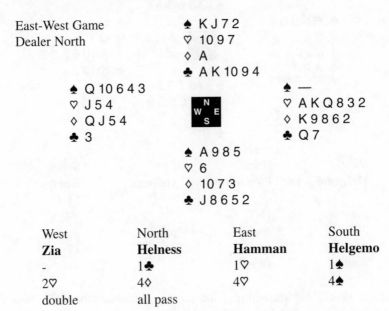

	♠ K J 7 2	
East-West Game	♥ 10 9 7	
Dealer North	◊ A	
	♣ A K 10 9 4	

♠ Q 10 6 4 3		♠ —
♥ J 5 4		♥ A K Q 8 3 2
◊ Q J 5 4		◊ K 9 8 6 2
♣ 3		♣ Q 7

	♠ A 9 8 5	
	♥ 6	
	◊ 10 7 3	
	♣ J 8 6 5 2	

West	North	East	South
Zia	**Helness**	**Hamman**	**Helgemo**
-	1♣	1♥	1♠
2♥	4◊	4♥	4♠
double	all pass		

Zia led a heart, Hamman winning with the queen. Had he continued with another heart, the contract would have been made. Declarer would ruff in the South hand, cash the ace of trumps and finesse the jack. He would then ruff his last heart in hand and play on clubs. When West ruffed he would be down to the same trump length as the dummy. Declarer would win a diamond exit to the ace, draw another round of trumps with the king, then return to the club suit. He would have won the battle for trump control.

The wily Bob Hamman could see all this in his crystal ball. At Trick 2 he switched to a diamond. Now the defenders would win the battle for control. When Zia gained the lead he could attack the dummy's trump length by playing on diamonds.

Sometimes a defender switches to a particular card with the aim of making life easy for partner. The next deal is from the 2000 Bermuda Bowl, Norway facing Indonesia in the quarter-finals. Geir sat West with Tor Helness East.

```
North-South Game          ♠ 10 8
Dealer South              ♡ K 4 3
                          ◇ Q 7 4
                          ♣ Q J 6 5 4
        ♠ A K 9 5 4                       ♠ 6
        ♡ 9 7                N            ♡ Q 10
        ◇ J 9 8           W     E         ◇ A 10 6 5 3 2
        ♣ A 9 3              S            ♣ K 10 7 2
                          ♠ Q J 7 3 2
                          ♡ A J 8 6 5 2
                          ◇ K
                          ♣ 8
```

West	North	East	South
Helgemo	**Panelewen**	**Helness**	**Karwur**
-	-	-	1♠
pass	1NT	2◇	2♡
3♡	double	pass	pass
4◇	pass	pass	4♡
double	all pass		

Geir's 3♡ cue bid showed a sound raise in diamonds, based on honour strength rather than distribution. Helness's subsequent pass over the double showed a weaker hand than a conversion to 4◇ would have done. The Indonesian South ended in four hearts doubled and the ◇8 lead was won by the ace. Suppose you had been East. What would you have played next?

It looks obvious to switch to the singleton spade and that is what most players would have done. Look at the problem this would have presented to West, though. What should he do after cashing two spades and the ace of clubs? Should he play another spade, hoping for a trump promotion, or should he try for a second club trick?

Helness foresaw this dilemma and made a surprising play at Trick 2. He cashed ♣K! The strong bidding opposite made it almost certain that partner held the club ace. Helness wanted to clarify the situation in the suit. Only after cashing the club, did he switch to a spade. Geir cashed two spade winners and on the second round Helness threw ♣2. This count signal, showing a residual holding of three clubs, confirmed what the bidding had already suggested – that declarer's shape was 5-6-1-1, rather than 5-5-1-2.

It was easy now for Geir to play a third spade. Declarer could have escaped for one down, by ruffing with the king and finessing against East's queen. Not expecting the trumps to lie as they did, he (carelessly, it seems) discarded a club. Helness ruffed with the 10 and the defenders picked up a valuable +500.

Norway faced USA in the semi-finals of the 1993 World Junior championships and Geir was for once on the receiving end. Len Holtz found a great defence in the West seat.

```
North-South Game        ♠ J 8 7
Dealer North            ♡ 10 9 6
                        ♢ A Q 10 7
                        ♣ J 5 2
      ♠ 10 5 4                        ♠ 9 2
      ♡ J                  N           ♡ A K 8 7 5
      ♢ K J 4 3 2       W   E         ♢ 8 6 5
      ♣ K Q 4 3           S           ♣ 10 9 7
                        ♠ A K Q 6 3
                        ♡ Q 4 3 2
                        ♢ 9
                        ♣ A 8 6
```

West	North	East	South
Holtz	**Aaseng**	**Ferro**	**Helgemo**
-	pass	2♡	2♠
pass	3♣	pass	4♠
all pass			

Holtz led ♡J and his partner cashed two winners in the suit. He ruffed a third round of hearts and then had a key play to make. What would you have done?

Suppose West switches to ♣K, as many defenders would. Geir would win with the ace, draw trumps, and cash his remaining winners in the majors. This end position would result:

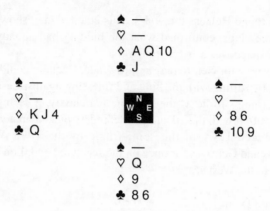

When ♡Q was played, West would be squeezed. If he threw a diamond, Geir would discard ♣J from dummy and score three diamond tricks. If instead West threw a club, Geir would throw ◊10 from dummy and finesse ◊Q for the contract.

This ending did not arise because at Trick 4 Holtz switched to a diamond! This killed a vital link to the dummy and the game could no longer be made.

A diamond switch was likely to give away the contract only when South held something like: ♠AKQ963 ♡Q432 ◊ — ♣A86. The free diamond finesse would then give him two club discards. With such a hand, however, Geir would surely have overcalled 3♠ rather than 2♠.

Geir himself made a similar entry-killing switch, during the 1996 Rhodes Olympiad.

Game All
Dealer West

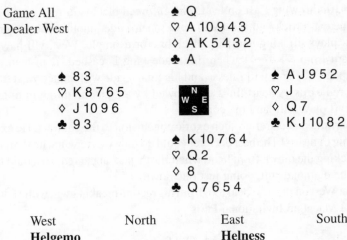

♠ Q
♡ A 10 9 4 3
◇ A K 5 4 3 2
♣ A

♠ 8 3
♡ K 8 7 6 5
◇ J 10 9 6
♣ 9 3

♠ A J 9 5 2
♡ J
◇ Q 7
♣ K J 10 8 2

♠ K 10 7 6 4
♡ Q 2
◇ 8
♣ Q 7 6 5 4

West	North	East	South
Helgemo		**Helness**	
pass	1◇	1♠	pass
pass	2♡	pass	3NT
all pass			

Geir led ♠8 to the queen and ace. Tor Helness then switched to ♣2, the low spotcard indicating interest in this suit. The trick was won by the bare ace in dummy and declarer then played ace, king and another diamond, throwing Geir on lead. This position had been reached:

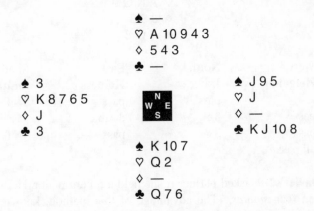

♠ —
♡ A 10 9 4 3
◇ 5 4 3
♣ —

♠ 3
♡ K 8 7 6 5
◇ J
♣ 3

♠ J 9 5
♡ J
◇ —
♣ K J 10 8

♠ K 10 7
♡ Q 2
◇ —
♣ Q 7 6

What should West do next? Suppose he switches to a low heart, South winning the jack with the queen. If declarer reads the position correctly he can

119

exit with ♠10, throwing East on lead. The enforced black-suit return will give declarer one extra trick and West will have to surrender another subsequently.

If East plays the king and jack of clubs, for example, West will have no good discard from ♡K87 ◊J when the spade king is cashed. If instead East returns a spade, declarer will finesse and his final spade will reduce West to the same four red cards. A heart finesse, followed by a diamond throw-in to force another heart play, will land the contract.

Geir permitted declarer no such exotic conclusion to the contract. He exited with the king of hearts! The best declarer could do now was to win with dummy's ace, unblocking the queen from hand when East's jack appeared. He could then establish the diamond suit, going just one down.

Geir sat West on the next deal too, from his record-breaking win with Helness in the 1998 Macallan Invitational Pairs.

```
Love All              ♠ Q J 9 7
Dealer North          ♡ 2
                      ◊ 10 7 6 4
                      ♣ 10 6 4 3
     ♠ K 8 3                              ♠ 6 5 2
     ♡ 10 8 7 6 5 4 3      N              ♡ J
     ◊ A K              W     E           ◊ Q 5 3 2
     ♣ 7                   S              ♣ K J 9 5 2
                      ♠ A 10 4
                      ♡ A K Q 9
                      ◊ J 9 8
                      ♣ A Q 8
```

West	North	East	South
Helgemo	**Davies**	**Helness**	**Smith**
-	pass	pass	2NT
pass	3♣	double	3◊
pass	3♡	pass	3NT
all pass			

Pat Davies's 3♣ asked partner if she held a 5-card major. Her subsequent 3♡ showed four *spades*. (The advantage of this method, known as Puppet Stayman, is that the strong hand will play the contract when a 4-4 fit is found.)

Geir led ♡6 to the jack and king. When Nicola Smith led ◊9, he won with the king and tried his luck with another heart. Helness showed out, throwing an

120

encouraging club, and declarer won with the nine. Now came a second diamond to Geir's ace.

The key moment had been reached. At some other tables West persisted with hearts now. This gave their declarer an easy time. He could knock out East's diamond queen and eventually cross in spades to take a club finesse. Geir decided that the moment had arrived for a club switch, which went to East's nine and South's queen.

Smith could now sense a danger to her contract. If she cleared the diamond suit, East would knock out her last club stopper (a club had been thrown from dummy). The game would then fail if East held the spade king as an entry to his long clubs.

Everything depended on the position of the spade king. If West held the card, it was safe to knock out the last diamond stopper. If East held it, the game could be made by playing a spade to the queen. East would have to duck, to kill the suit, but declarer could then score three spade tricks by finessing on the return.

Recalling that Geir had not entered the auction, despite holding a seven-card heart suit and ◊A K, declarer placed the spade king with East. A spade to the queen held the trick, but the contract could no longer be made. She took a losing finesse of ♣10 and the game was one down.

Newcomers to the game learn at an early stage to lead high from a doubleton. As the years go by, exceptions to this rule may arise. On the next deal – from the Open Pairs at the 1999 Spring Nationals in Vancouver – Tony Forrester led low from a doubleton at Trick 1. Geir won the trick and led low from a doubleton of his own on the next trick! Let's see what the effect was.

Game All   ♠ K J 7 6 5
Dealer North   ♡ 7 5
         ◇ A Q 5 4
         ♣ K 7

  ♠ Q 3   ♠ A 9 8 4 2
  ♡ A J 6   ♡ 9 4 2
  ◇ K 9 6 2   N   ◇ J 3
  ♣ A J 10 3   W   E   ♣ 9 6 4
         S

        ♠ 10
        ♡ K Q 10 8 3
        ◇ 10 8 7
        ♣ Q 8 5 2

West	North	East	South
Forrester		**Helgemo**	
-	1♠	pass	1NT
double	2◇	pass	2♡
all pass			

Forrester had a singularly unattractive lead in the unbid suit – clubs. Nor did a red-suit lead look promising. He decided to lead dummy's suit and chose ♠3 (the queen would have worked better, as it happens).

Declarer played low from dummy and Geir won with the ace. Some defenders would now have tried to give partner a spade ruff. Geir recalled the bidding, however. If South held ♠Q10, he would surely have given preference to 2♠. Placing partner with the spade queen, Geir switched to ◇3. South's eight was covered by the nine and dummy's queen. Forrester won the king of clubs with the ace and returned a low diamond. Now we see the advantage of Geir's 'low from a doubleton' at Trick 2! Had the jack been played to dummy's queen, West could not have continued the suit.

Not surprisingly, declarer had read East's earlier ◇3 as a singleton. He ducked this second round of diamonds and Geir scored a trick with the jack. When he returned ♠9, declarer threw a club and the trick was won in dummy. A club to the queen was followed by a club ruff in dummy and a trump to the king and ace. The king of diamonds was covered by dummy's ace and ruffed by East. Geir now played a third spade, which would have promoted the setting trick even if West had started with A-10-6 in the trump suit, rather than A-J-6.

When you play at your local club, you often escape any minor inaccuracies in your play. This is not true at the top level, as Italy's Norberto Bocchi found out on the next deal, played against Norway in the quarter finals of the 1997 Bermuda Bowl.

Game All   ♠ A J 9 8
Dealer East   ♡ K 8 3 2
    ◊ 4
    ♣ J 9 7 3

♠ K 10 4 3   ♠ Q 7 6
♡ 9 7 6   ♡ 5
◊ Q 9 8 3   ◊ K 10 6 5 2
♣ 10 5   ♣ A K 6 4

    ♠ 5 2
    ♡ A Q J 10 4
    ◊ A J 7
    ♣ Q 8 2

West	North	East	South
Helgemo	**Duboin**	**Helness**	**Bocchi**
-	-	1◊	1♡
2◊	3◊	pass	4♡
all pass			

Once again, the cue-bid (by North) showed a sound raise in partner's suit. Geir led a diamond to the king and ace. Bocchi now erred by cashing the ace of trumps before ruffing a diamond. He returned to the trump queen, finding the suit 3-1, then ruffed his last diamond. Stuck inconveniently in the dummy, he had to broach the clubs while there was still a trump out.

Tor Helness rose with the king of clubs and the critical moment for the defence had been reached. It would not be good enough to cash his second club winner and give West a club ruff. Dummy's fourth club would then provide declarer with a discard of his losing spade. Helness made no mistake. He switched to a spade, West's king forcing the ace. When a second club was played, Helness took his ace and gave partner a club ruff. The spade queen was the setting trick.

At the other table Glenn Groetheim received the same opening lead to 4♡. He ruffed a diamond immediately, returned to a trump, and ruffed a second diamond. After drawing trumps, he took a successful view in clubs (low towards the queen) and made the game easily.

We move now to the 1998 Generali World Individual championship. Geir sat East and his partner for the following deal was the Russian, Kholomeev.

East-West Game
Dealer East

```
                    ♠ J 6
                    ♡ A J 10 8 3
                    ◊ Q 6 2
                    ♣ K J 8
♠ 5 4 3 2                           ♠ K Q 10 8 7
♡ Q 5              N                ♡ K 9 6 2
◊ J            W       E            ◊ K 9 7
♣ 10 9 7 5 3 2        S             ♣ A
                    ♠ A 9
                    ♡ 7 4
                    ◊ A 10 8 5 4 3
                    ♣ Q 6 4
```

West	North	East	South
Kholomeev	**Chemla**	**Helgemo**	**Freeman**
-	-	1♠	2◊
pass	2♡	pass	3◊
3♣	4◊	all pass	

West led a spade and Dick Freeman won with the ace, exiting with his remaining spade. Suppose you had been East. How would you have defended from this point?

Geir cashed the ace of clubs, then switched to the king of hearts! This spectacular play is known as a Deschapelles Coup. The aim is to blast a way through to partner's queen of hearts (if he holds the card).

Freeman won with dummy's heart ace and led the queen of trumps, covered by the king and ace. When West's jack appeared, the lie of the trump suit was evident. Declarer tried to get back to dummy with a club, to finesse against East's nine of trumps. Geir ruffed and crossed to partner's queen of hearts to receive a second ruff. Two down!

At another table the play in 4◊ started in the same way. Claude Delmouly of France found the brilliant Deschapelles Coup but failed to cash the ace of clubs first. Kowalski, the Polish declarer, won with the ace of hearts and also played the queen of trumps, drawing the king, ace and jack. This was the position:

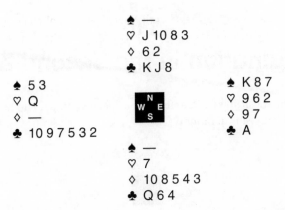

```
              ♠ —
              ♡ J 10 8 3
              ◇ 6 2
              ♣ K J 8
♠ 5 3                        ♠ K 8 7
♡ Q              N           ♡ 9 6 2
◇ —           W     E        ◇ 9 7
♣ 10 9 7 5 3 2   S           ♣ A
              ♠ —
              ♡ 7
              ◇ 10 8 5 4 3
              ♣ Q 6 4
```

Declarer played a club now, trying to reach dummy, and subsequently suffered a club ruff for one down. Suppose he had played a heart to West's queen instead, aiming to break the link between the defenders' hands. After a club to the ace East would be endplayed, forced to give declarer a free finesse in the trump suit or to concede an entry to dummy. The contract would then be made.

Now we can see why it was necessary for Geir to cash the ace of clubs. His magical sequence – ace of clubs, king of hearts – was the only way to beat the contract against best declarer play.

11
Imagination in the Second Seat

Suppose you are sitting East, defending a spade contract, and have this view of the club side suit in dummy:

♣ A J 8 6 4 3

     ♣ K 5

Declarer calls for ♣3. Do you win with the king? Most defenders would do so without much thought, but it is not always best. Geir faced such a situation on this deal from the quarter-finals of the 1997 Bermuda Bowl, played in Tunisia:

```
North-South Game      ♠ J 3 2
Dealer East           ♡ 9 8 7 6
                      ◇ —
                      ♣ A J 8 6 4 3
      ♠ K 6                              ♠ 10 9 5
      ♡ K 10 3                           ♡ 5 4 2
      ◇ A 6 5 3 2                        ◇ K Q 9 7 4
      ♣ Q 9 2                            ♣ K 5
                      ♠ A Q 8 7 4
                      ♡ A Q J
                      ◇ J 10 8
                      ♣ 10 7
```

West	North	East	South
Helness	**Lauria**	**Helgemo**	**Versace**
-	-	pass	1♠
double	2♣	3◇	pass
pass	3♠	all pass	

Helness led the ace of diamonds, ruffed in the dummy. 'Small club,' said Versace.

Geir played low, without a flicker, and Helness captured South's ten with the queen. After some thought, Helness returned another club. Versace finessed to the bare king and Geir now switched to a trump. Helness won with the king and played a second trump to dummy's bare jack. Geir still had a trump to deal with the ace of clubs, so declarer had to lose a heart and two more diamonds! That was two down and an 8-IMP swing when the same contract was made at the other table.

On the next deal, from the 1998 Vanderbilt, it was West who held K-x in the key suit. Both declarers reached the same contract of six diamonds and all depended on West's reaction at Trick 2!

Love All   ♠ Q 10 8
Dealer South   ♡ 10 5
                 ◊ A Q 5 2
                 ♣ K J 5 2

♠ K 2		♠ J 9 7 6 5
♡ Q 7	N	♡ 9 4 2
◊ 10 6 3	W E	◊ 8 4
♣ A 9 8 6 4 3	S	♣ Q 10 7

                 ♠ A 4 3
                 ♡ A K J 8 6 3
                 ◊ K J 9 7
                 ♣ —

West	North	East	South
Helgemo		**Forrester**	
-	-	-	1♡
pass	2♣	pass	2◊
pass	3◊	pass	3♡
pass	3NT	pass	6◊
all pass			

Geir led a small trump, won in the South hand. Even if both red suits break 3-2 and declarer can ruff the hearts good, he still has to avoid two spade losers. If declarer is going to lead a spade towards dummy, guessing which card to play, when do you think is the right time to do it?

On some contracts it is best to delay the decision as long as possible. By then, you may have discovered more about the defenders' hands. That is hardly likely here. Indeed, there is considerable advantage to be gained by playing a spade immediately, at Trick 2. When West holds the king and not the jack, he will be put to a tricky decision before he knows much about the hand. If declarer has a loser elsewhere, it would be right to grab the king. The pressure on West is all the greater because he will not have been expecting declarer to lead a spade so early.

Both declarers in the Vanderbilt found the strong move of a spade at Trick 2. Geir played a cool ♠2 from the West seat and declarer called for dummy's 10, losing to the jack. Forrester returned a trump, won in the dummy. Declarer then ran ♡10, hoping to set up the hearts without using dummy's fourth trump. (It would then be possible to throw a spade from dummy and ruff declarer's third spade.) His luck was out. Geir won with the heart queen and the contract was one down. At the other table declarer's ploy of an early spade drew blood. West rose with the king and the contract was made by ruffing the hearts good.

You may have noticed that declarer missed a small extra chance. Before crossing to dummy to take the heart finesse, he should have cashed ♠A. When the spade king fell, dummy's fourth trump would become available for ruffing the heart suit good.

Ducking smoothly in such circumstances is possible only if you have 'been there before'. There is little time for calculation because a hesitation will reveal the position of the king. Two inferences were clear on this particular deal, however. First, declarer would not make such a spade play unless he was void in clubs; if you grab the spade king, there is no chance whatever that the club ace will be a second defensive trick. Second, declarer cannot hold the spade jack or he would be finessing through East. This is the key inference. If you play low smoothly, declarer is very likely to try dummy's 10.

12

Imaginative Drawing of Trumps in Defence

Then you're defending, do you find it easy to know whether you should play on trumps? Apart from a few standard situations, you can rarely be sure that a trump opening lead is right. Once the dummy is down, though, the decision should be easier (if it is not too late!).

The following deal contributed to a victory in the Board-a-Match championship at the 1999 Boston Fall Nationals.

Love All
Dealer West

	♠ 10 9 7 6 4	
	♡ A J 6	
	◊ Q	
	♣ A 6 4 3	
♠ A K J 8 3		♠ 2
♡ 5	N W E S	♡ 10 7 3
◊ A K 10 9 3		◊ J 8 7 6
♣ Q 8		♣ J 9 7 5 2
	♠ Q 5	
	♡ K Q 9 8 4 2	
	◊ 5 4 2	
	♣ K 10	

West	North	East	South
Helgemo		**Forrester**	
1♠	pass	pass	2♡
3◊	3♡	4◊	pass
pass	4♡	pass	pass
double	all pass		

Tony Forrester nudged the opponents up one more level and Geir was happy to double. A singleton trump lead was not attractive and Geir led ♠A. When the dummy appeared, with its singleton diamond, a trump switch was indicated.

Declarer won East's ♥7 with ♥8 and played a diamond. Geir had to win this, unfortunately for the defence, and had no further trump to play. Needing to find an entry to partner's hand, he exited with a low spade. When Forrester ruffed and played a second trump, declarer was left with an unavoidable second loser in diamonds. One down.

Board-a-match can be a cruel game. At the other table East and West found the same splendid defence to beat 4♥. Sadly for them, they had omitted to double the contract!

In 1997 Geir won the Politiken World Pairs, partnering Krzyztof Martens of Poland. The defenders badly needed to play on trumps when this deal arose:

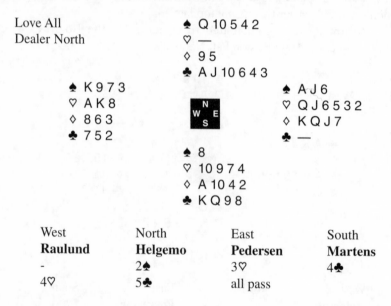

Love All
Dealer North

	♠ Q 10 5 4 2	
	♥ —	
	◊ 9 5	
	♣ A J 10 6 4 3	
♠ K 9 7 3		♠ A J 6
♥ A K 8		♥ Q J 6 5 3 2
◊ 8 6 3		◊ K Q J 7
♣ 7 5 2		♣ —
	♠ 8	
	♥ 10 9 7 4	
	◊ A 10 4 2	
	♣ K Q 9 8	

West	North	East	South
Raulund	**Helgemo**	**Pedersen**	**Martens**
-	2♠	3♥	4♣
4♥	5♣	all pass	

Geir's Polish 2♠ opening showed a hand of limited strength, containing spades and an unspecified minor. Martens' response of 4♣ indicated that he was willing to play at the four level in partner's minor suit. East-West could make at least eleven tricks in hearts, as you see, but West understandably devalued his king of spades.

There is only one lead that definitely beats the club game – a trump! West could expect South to be short in spades and should probably have diagnosed that a trump lead was best. He actually led the king of hearts, ruffed in the dummy. Hoping to set up a crossruff, Martens now called for a low spade. East was in a difficult situation. To beat the contract, he needed to play the six. West

130

could then win the trick and play a (somewhat belated) trump. However, if declarer had the bare spade king and West held the ace of diamonds, it would be essential to rise with the ace of spades and switch to diamonds. East rose with the spade ace (it's hard to blame him) and switched to the queen of diamonds.

Martens was hoping to take four spade ruffs in his hand. Since heart ruffs in the dummy would give him only three entries for this, he would need a diamond ruff entry too. He therefore ducked the queen of diamonds. If East's diamonds were headed by the queen-jack, and West overtook with the king to play a trump, declarer's ◊A10 would then be worth two tricks.

As the cards lay, any chance of beating the game had already departed. Martens won the diamond continuation and smartly added ten more tricks on a crossruff. Game made.

We mentioned in our opening to this chapter that there are some situations that call for a trump lead. We have already seen one of these – when the opponents are heavily outgunned in terms of points and have sacrificed in the hope of scoring lots of trump tricks. Another such situation is when an opponent has shown a 4-4-4-1 hand, or close to it, and his partner has chosen to play in one of the suits at a low level.

A strong example of this arose in the 1994 Cap Volmac World Top pairs. Geir and Tor Helness faced the American maestros, Jeff Meckstroth and Eric Rodwell.

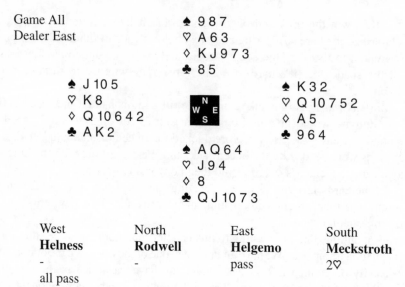

Game All   ♠ 9 8 7
Dealer East   ♡ A 6 3
               ◊ K J 9 7 3
               ♣ 8 5

♠ J 10 5   ♠ K 3 2
♡ K 8   ♡ Q 10 7 5 2
◊ Q 10 6 4 2   ◊ A 5
♣ A K 2   ♣ 9 6 4

               ♠ A Q 6 4
               ♡ J 9 4
               ◊ 8
               ♣ Q J 10 7 3

West	North	East	South
Helness	**Rodwell**	**Helgemo**	**Meckstroth**
-	-	pass	2♡
all pass			

Jeff Meckstroth's 2♡ was a version of the Precision 2◊ opening, showing a three-suited hand in the 10-15 points range, short in diamonds.

Tor Helness knew that a trump lead was usually effective against such bidding and was not deflected from this course by his unattractive holding in the suit. Boldly, he led the king of trumps. Meckstroth misguessed, ducking in the dummy. A second round of trumps ran to Geir's queen and he played a third round, clearing the suit. Meckstroth could not avoid going four down now and the resultant -400 cost the Americans a full 10 IMPs against the datum score on the board.

13
Imaginative Defence in the Endgame

It is rare for a good declarer to defend weakly when it comes to the endgame. Why is that? It's because understanding the various endplays and squeeze positions from declarer's point of view allows you calculate how they can be thwarted. If you understand the entry situation necessary to achieve a certain type of squeeze, you have a better chance of destroying the play when defending.

West faced a difficult task, defending this hand played by Geir in the 1997 Blue Ribbon Pairs in St Louis. See if you can spot the chance he missed, as the play is described.

```
East-West Game          ♠ A 10 8 7
Dealer West             ♡ A J 5 4
                        ◊ 7 6 2
                        ♣ Q 9
   ♠ K Q 5 4                             ♠ J 2
   ♡ Q 6 3 2              N              ♡ K 10 9 8 7
   ◊ 3              W         E          ◊ A J 10 9 4
   ♣ 10 5 3 2             S              ♣ J
                        ♠ 9 6 3
                        ♡ —
                        ◊ K Q 8 5
                        ♣ A K 8 7 6 4
```

West	North	East	South
	Forrester		**Helgemo**
pass	pass	1♡	2♣
3♣	double	3♡	4♣
double	all pass		

You could have guessed it was a Pairs hand from West's final double! West led his singleton diamond. East won with the ace and returned ◊J, covered by the king and ruffed. West returned a trump, to the jack and king, and Geir crossed to dummy with the queen of trumps.

How could declarer possibly avoid losing two more tricks, you may be asking yourself. We will see! Geir called for a low heart from dummy at Trick 5 and East went in with the king. This was a bad mistake. Even if West's heart raise is ignored, it was clear that declarer had a void heart. He would obviously not allow East to gain the lead when another diamond ruff was sure to follow.

Geir ruffed in the South hand, then played three more rounds of trumps. This end position arose:

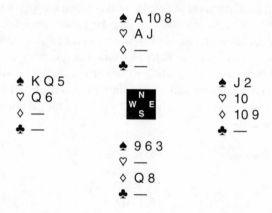

```
              ♠ A 10 8
              ♡ A J
              ◊ —
              ♣ —
  ♠ K Q 5                    ♠ J 2
  ♡ Q 6          N           ♡ 10
  ◊ —          W   E         ◊ 10 9
  ♣ —            S           ♣ —
              ♠ 9 6 3
              ♡ —
              ◊ Q 8
              ♣ —
```

What could West throw on ◊Q? A heart would give the dummy two tricks in the suit. He actually chose to discard ♣5. Geir threw ♡J from dummy, then played ace and another spade. West had to win and surrender the last two tricks to the dummy.

It would not be good enough for West to throw a spade honour in the five-card ending shown. Declarer would throw ♡J from dummy, as before, then lead a spade. If West played low, declarer could win with dummy's ace and surrender a second round of spades to the safe hand. If instead West played his remaining honour, he would be left on lead.

Look at any collection of successful squeezes and you will be amazed how many of them could have been defeated by an attack on declarer's communications. Nearly all squeezes require a threat card that is accompanied by an entry. The ◊10 is the threat card in these two basic forms:

(1)   ◊ A 10   (2)   ◊ A 5

         ◊ 5   ◊ K 10 3

Type (1) is the most familiar and is adequate when the squeeze card is opposite the threat card. Type (2) is needed when the squeeze card is in the same hand as the threat card. In both cases, the defenders may be able to break the squeeze if they can play on the suit involved, removing a key entry.

The next deal, from the 1994 Cap Volmac World Top pairs, is an example of this:

Love All
Dealer East

♠ Q J 7 6
♡ J 8 7
◊ 9 5
♣ Q J 9 7

♠ 10 9 4 3   ♠ A 8
♡ 4   ♡ K Q 6 5 3 2
◊ A Q 8 6 4   ◊ 2
♣ K 8 6   ♣ 5 4 3 2

♠ K 5 2
♡ A 10 9
◊ K J 10 7 3
♣ A 10

West	North	East	South
Westra	**Helness**	**Leufkens**	**Helgemo**
-	-	2♡	2NT
pass	3NT	all pass	

A 2NT overcall of a weak-two is usually based on more than 15 points. Geir assessed his hand as being worth nearer 17 points, with all those intermediate cards. Westra led ◊6 against the notrump game and Geir won with the seven. He continued with the ace and 10 of clubs, West winning with the king. The heart switch went to East's queen and Geir allowed this card to hold.

The first key moment for the defence had been reached. Suppose East plays a low heart next, giving declarer an entry to dummy. The contract will easily be made. Declarer will cash dummy's clubs, finding that East has 2-6-1-4 shape, then lead a low spade through East's ace doubleton. He can subsequently duck a spade to the ace, setting up three spade tricks for a total of nine. Leufkens found the one card in his hand that would allow the contract to be beaten. He exited with the *king* of hearts, to force declarer to win in the South hand. So far so good, for the defence.

Geir won with the ace of hearts and led a spade to the queen and ace. East was on lead and this was the position:

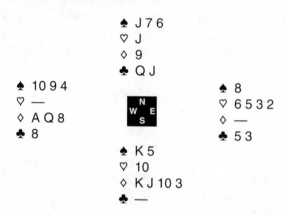

```
            ♠ J 7 6
            ♡ J
            ◊ 9
            ♣ Q J
♠ 10 9 4                    ♠ 8
♡ —            N            ♡ 6 5 3 2
◊ A Q 8      W   E          ◊ —
♣ 8            S            ♣ 5 3
            ♠ K 5
            ♡ 10
            ◊ K J 10 3
            ♣ —
```

This was the second key moment for the defence. Leufkens in fact returned a heart. Geir won in the dummy and cashed two clubs, throwing diamonds from his hand. West, who needed to keep all his spades, was forced to bare the ace of diamonds. Geir could then establish a ninth trick for himself in diamonds and the game was made.

Look back to the seven-card end position. The spade holding is an example of the Type (2) threat that we noted earlier. Had East returned a spade, he would have killed a vital entry. The game would have been beaten.

Finally, suppose West had led a low spade against 3NT. The defenders would then have had scope for a piece of excellent communications play. East must play the eight! If declarer then clears the clubs, West must play a heart while East still has the spade ace as an entry to cash his heart winner.

Suppose, instead, that declarer is inspired enough to duck a spade to the bare ace at Trick 2. A diamond to the queen, followed by a heart switch, will still beat the contract. Although East is out of the action, declarer cannot untangle his tricks in the minors.

In 1998 Tor Helness and Geir won the Macallan Invitational Pairs by a record margin. (They scored 693 VPs to the second pair's 539.) This was the very first hand of the event:

```
Love All                ♠ A K Q 7 6 5 2
Dealer North            ♡ A 6
                        ◊ —
                        ♣ K 8 6 4
     ♠ 10                              ♠ J 9 8 4
     ♡ Q 7 5          N                ♡ 4 2
     ◊ A K Q 6      W   E              ◊ 9 8 5 4 3
     ♣ Q J 9 7 3       S               ♣ 10 2
                        ♠ 3
                        ♡ K J 10 9 8 3
                        ◊ J 10 7 2
                        ♣ A 5
```

West	North	East	South
Helgemo	**Mittelman**	**Helness**	**Gordon**
-	2♣	pass	2♠
pass	3♠	pass	4♡
pass	4♠	pass	4NT
pass	5♣	pass	5♡
pass	6♠	all pass	

Diana Gordon's 2♠ response showed three controls. 4NT was Roman Keycard Blackwood, with spades agreed as trumps, and North's 5♣ response showed three key cards (♠AK ♡A). Gordon's 5♡ asked for the trump queen. Holding that card, Mittelman jumped to the spade slam. Because of the artificial response on the first round, the contract would be played by South.

Geir led ◊A, ruffed in the dummy. Gordon could have made the contract by playing four rounds of trumps, ruffing the hearts good when she regained the lead. Instead, she played ace, king and another club. Helness discarded and she ruffed with the three. The ◊10 was covered with the king and ruffed. Declarer then played four rounds of trumps, throwing East on lead. Geir, meanwhile, had discarded a club, a heart (unguarding the queen) and a diamond. It was Helness (East) to play in this end position:

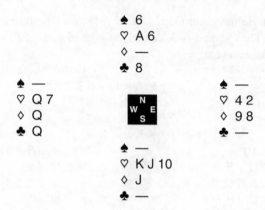

Helness played ♡2, covered by the jack, seven and ace. Declarer now had to guess what to do in hearts. Not expecting Geir to have unguarded the heart queen so early in the play, she eventually opted for a finesse of the 10. Geir won with the queen and cashed a club trick, putting the slam two down.

14
Imagination in the Third Seat

Your partner makes the opening lead, a card is played from dummy, and it is your turn to play in the third seat. The rule handed out to beginners is clear-cut: 'Third hand high unless you have cards that surround a high card in dummy'. Yes, but there are several exceptions to this and the defender must sometimes use his... what's the word? Ah yes, imagination.

Our first deal comes from the 1999 Reisinger, a point-a-board event.

```
North-South Game          ♠ K J 10 9 6 3
Dealer South              ♡ 9 7 4
                          ◇ 7 2
                          ♣ 6 5
        ♠ 7 5 4                              ♠ A Q 8 2
        ♡ K J 8 5          N                 ♡ 10 3 2
        ◇ 9 8 6 3        W   E               ◇ A J 5
        ♣ 8 3              S                 ♣ A K 4
                          ♠ —
                          ♡ A Q 6
                          ◇ K Q 10 4
                          ♣ Q J 10 9 7 2
```

West	North	East	South
Forrester		**Helgemo**	
-	-	-	1♣
pass	1♠	1NT	double
pass	2♠	pass	3♣
all pass			

Playing third and fifth leads, Forrester led ◇6. Suppose you had been East. How would you have defended?

Nearly every defender in the world would win with the ace and *then* start to think! Geir put in the effort before playing to the first trick. There were 18 points between the two closed hands and South's double of 1NT suggested he would hold nearly all of them. The odds were therefore higher than normal that South held the king and queen of diamonds. What was more, there were no entries to dummy. If East withheld the diamond ace, declarer could win this trick but would not be able to lead towards his remaining diamond holding.

Reasoning in this way, Geir played the jack of diamonds at Trick 1! Declarer could score only four trump tricks, two diamond tricks and the heart ace. Two down and +200 to East-West.

At the other table a world-class player sat East. The contract and opening lead were the same but he rose with the diamond ace at Trick 1. Declarer now had three diamond tricks and escaped for one down – a winning board

When defending at notrumps, you may choose to withhold a high card for a different reason. You want to knock out one of declarer's stoppers. Geir was partnered by Tom Johansen on this deal from a 1991 pairs tournament in Bergen:

Love All
Dealer West

```
                    ♠ J 8 7 4
                    ♡ A 6
                    ◇ Q 6 4 2
                    ♣ Q 9 6
   ♠ K 9 6                          ♠ A 5 2
   ♡ 8 4              N             ♡ K J 10 9 7
   ◇ K 10 9 7 5 3   W   E           ◇ 8
   ♣ 7 5              S             ♣ 10 8 4 3
                    ♠ Q 10 3
                    ♡ Q 5 3 2
                    ◇ A J
                    ♣ A K J 2
```

West	North	East	South
Johansen		**Helgemo**	
pass	pass	2♡	2NT
pass	3NT	all pass	

Johansen led ♡8 and declarer played low from dummy. Suppose you had been East. How would you have defended?

Reading his partner for a doubleton heart, Geir aimed to remove one of declarer's heart stoppers while partner still had a heart to play. He played ♡9 at Trick 1. Declarer won with the queen and led a low spade from his hand. Johansen knew what to do! He rose with the king and cleared partner's heart suit. When declarer persisted with spades, Geir won with the ace and cashed three hearts to put the game one down.

You can see what would happen if Geir won the first trick with the king, continuing the suit. West would have no hearts left when he came on lead in spades. The contract would easily be made.

What if declarer allows East's ♡9 to win the first trick? That's no good. East can switch to a diamond, or clear a second heart trick for himself and later switch to a diamond. Either way, that will be five tricks for the defence.

There were two elements to Geir's surprising third-hand play on the next deal, from the 1997 Macallan Invitation Pairs – discovery and deception. His opponents were the Americans, Nick Nickell and Dick Freeman.

East-West Game   ♠ A J 9 5 4
Dealer East   ♡ 9 3
                  ◊ A 10 7 2
                  ♣ K 6

♠ K 10 7   ♠ Q 8 2
♡ 10 8   N   ♡ K J 6 2
◊ 8 6 5 3   W   E   ◊ K J 4
♣ Q 9 5 3   S   ♣ J 7 4

                  ♠ 6 3
                  ♡ A Q 7 5 4
                  ◊ Q 9
                  ♣ A 10 8 2

West	North	East	South
Helness	**Freeman**	**Helgemo**	**Nickell**
-	-	pass	1♡
pass	1♠	pass	2♣
pass	2◊	pass	2NT
pass	3NT	all pass	

Tor Helness led ◊5 (third and fifth leads) and declarer called for a low card from the dummy. Geir played the jack!

What was the purpose of such a play? Firstly, he would discover who held the diamond queen. If the jack won the trick, Geir would know that his partner held the queen. Also, West would then know that Geir held the king. A further possible advantage was that if the jack lost to the queen, declarer would subsequently misplace the king of diamonds. This is what actually happened as the play developed.

Nickell won the first trick with the diamond queen and led a low heart to West's ten. He won the club switch with the king in dummy and finessed the queen of hearts successfully. Ace and another heart set up a long card and Geir returned ♣J. Declarer won with the ace, cashed his long heart, and ran ♡9, preparing to claim the contract. Not so fast! When Geir won with the king of diamonds and returned a club, the defenders had five tricks.

Later in the same match another entertaining hand arose:

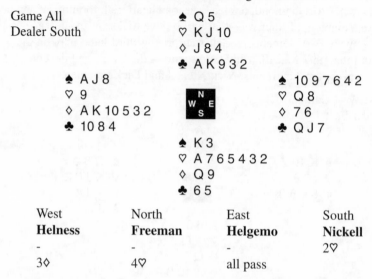

Game All   ♠ Q 5
Dealer South   ♡ K J 10
                 ◊ J 8 4
                 ♣ A K 9 3 2

♠ A J 8   ♠ 10 9 7 6 4 2
♡ 9   ♡ Q 8
◊ A K 10 5 3 2   ◊ 7 6
♣ 10 8 4   ♣ Q J 7

                 ♠ K 3
                 ♡ A 7 6 5 4 3 2
                 ◊ Q 9
                 ♣ 6 5

West	North	East	South
Helness	**Freeman**	**Helgemo**	**Nickell**
-	-	-	2♡
3◊	4♡	all pass	

Tor Helness cashed two top diamonds, followed by the ace of spades. When Geir denied interest in spades, signalling with the two, Helness continued with a third round of diamonds. If declarer had held only six trumps, with Geir holding ♡Q82, this would have promoted the setting trick by force. East would ruff with the eight, dislodging declarer's ace, and the trump queen would now be certain to score.

As it was, the situation looked hopeless for the defence. If Geir refused to ruff, declarer would surely pick up the trumps even he held only six trumps to the ace. With a 6-2 differential in diamonds, he would play the king on the first round, preparing for a finesse against East. Ruffing with the queen was clearly useless. How about ruffing with the eight? Yes, thought Geir, if West held ♡9-x declarer would then have a guess to make.

Geir duly ruffed the third round of diamonds with the eight. Nickell overruffed with the ace and now had a guess to make even though he had started with a seven-card trump suit. He led a low card towards dummy, the nine appearing from West. Had East ruffed with a singleton eight, or had he ruffed with the eight from Q-8?

It would end the chapter with a bang if we could tell you that Nickell finessed into the bare queen. No, the American master eventually read the position correctly, rising with the king and making his game.

You can't win them all!

15
Imaginative Communications
Play in Defence

When defending, you have two major tasks in the area of communications. You must keep in touch with your partner, so you can reach each other's hand to cash winners, to give ruffs, or to attack a suit from the right side. You must also do your utmost to sabotage declarer's communications.

On the next deal, from the 1996 Schiphol tournament in Amsterdam, Geir was allowed to make four hearts. Watch as the play is described and see if you can spot how the defenders might have beaten the contract.

North-South Game
Dealer North

	♠ 10 9 8 5	
	♡ K J 5	
	◊ J 10 3	
	♣ Q J 7	
♠ A K Q 6 4		♠ J 3 2
♡ 4 3	N W E S	♡ A 9 8
◊ A 7		◊ Q 8 6 5 4
♣ 10 4 3 2		♣ 8 5
	♠ 7	
	♡ Q 10 7 6 2	
	◊ K 9 2	
	♣ A K 9 6	

West	North	East	South
Russyan	**Helness**	**Sobolowska**	**Helgemo**
-	pass	pass	1♡
1♠	2♡	pass	2♣
double	4♡	all pass	

West played two top spades, Geir ruffing the second round. A trump went to the king and ace and East returned ♠J, forcing declarer to ruff. A club to the queen was followed by the jack of diamonds, covered by the queen, king and ace. A fourth spade forced Geir to ruff with the 10. He cashed the bare queen of trumps, crossed to ◊J, and drew East's last trump with the jack. Ten tricks!

Did you spot the defenders' error? East should not have covered the jack of diamonds. The jack runs to West's ace and when the fourth round of spades is led East can throw her remaining club. After cashing the queen of trumps, Geir would then have had no entry to dummy to draw the last trump.

Norway faced the Netherlands in the final of the 1993 Bermuda Bowl. Jansen and Westerhof defended sensationally against Geir's team mates on this 3NT deal:

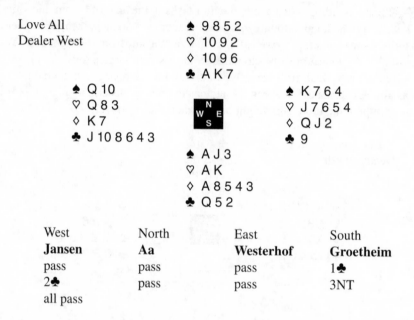

Love All
Dealer West

```
                    ♠ 9 8 5 2
                    ♡ 10 9 2
                    ◇ 10 9 6
                    ♣ A K 7
♠ Q 10                              ♠ K 7 6 4
♡ Q 8 3              N              ♡ J 7 6 5 4
◇ K 7            W       E          ◇ Q J 2
♣ J 10 8 6 4 3      S              ♣ 9
                    ♠ A J 3
                    ♡ A K
                    ◇ A 8 5 4 3
                    ♣ Q 5 2
```

West	North	East	South
Jansen	**Aa**	**Westerhof**	**Groetheim**
pass	pass	pass	1♣
2♣	pass	pass	3NT
all pass			

Glenn Groetheim opened a strong club and his partner's pass over the intervention showed 6-8 points. With a weaker hand North would have doubled. On a club lead (found at the other table, and at both tables of the Venice Cup final), declarer had time to establish the diamonds and the game was made. Piet Jansen made the inspired lead of ♡3. When Groetheim called for dummy's 10, Westerhof kept a firm hold of his jack (an essential move) and played an encouraging seven.

Groetheim won with the king and led a low diamond to the 10 and jack. Westerhof returned a low heart to declarer's ace and Jansen now unblocked the queen. Declarer had little option but to clear the diamonds and the moment had finally come for Westerhof to play his jack of hearts. Two more hearts followed and that was 10 IMPs to Holland.

When Norway faced Pakistan, on this deal from the 1992 Olympiad in Salsamaggiore, Glenn Groetheim and Geir had to be mindful of their own communications.

```
North-South Game        ♠ J 9 4
Dealer South            ♡ K 8 4 2
                        ◊ K J 6 5
                        ♣ 8 4
    ♠ Q 10 7 5                        ♠ K 8 6 3
    ♡ 10 9 6 5          N             ♡ J 3
    ◊ A 10 2        W       E         ◊ 9 7 3
    ♣ 10 3             S             ♣ A 9 7 5
                        ♠ A 2
                        ♡ A Q 7
                        ◊ Q 8 4
                        ♣ K Q J 6 2
```

West	North	East	South
Helgemo	**Nishat**	**Groetheim**	**Zia**
-	-	-	1NT
pass	2♣	pass	2◊
pass	3NT	all pass	

Geir led a third-and-fifth ♠7 to the nine, king and ace. Zia could see two likely spade tricks and three certain heart tricks. Since the club suit might yield four tricks and the diamonds could produce only three, he led ♣K at Trick 2. Groetheim took the ace immediately and returned ♠3 to Geir's queen.

At Trick 4 Geir played ♠10 (!) to North's jack. Had Zia been certain that the spades had started 4-4, he could simply have played on diamonds now. He played two more rounds of clubs, however, finding that the suit did not break. He then had to turn to the diamond suit. Geir rose with the ace and – thanks to his earlier unblock of the 10 – was able to lead the five of spades to his partner's eight. Groetheim scored ♣9 as the defenders' fifth trick.

Even when you look at all four hands on the next deal, from the 1998 Norwegian Premier League, it is not at all obvious how declarer could possibly fail in four hearts. He would have done, though, if West had not missed a clever move halfway through the play. See if you can spot the chance that Geir's partner overlooked.

Love All
Dealer South

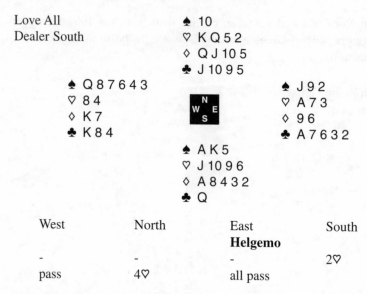

♠ 10
♡ K Q 5 2
♢ Q J 10 5
♣ J 10 9 5

♠ Q 8 7 6 4 3   ♠ J 9 2
♡ 8 4   ♡ A 7 3
♢ K 7   ♢ 9 6
♣ K 8 4   ♣ A 7 6 3 2

♠ A K 5
♡ J 10 9 6
♢ A 8 4 3 2
♣ Q

West	North	East	South
		Helgemo	
-	-	-	2♡
pass	4♡	all pass	

South's 2♡ opening showed four hearts and five diamonds and a hand in the 11-15 point range. West led ♣4 and declarer captured East's jack with the ace. Geir ducked the first round of trumps and won the second. He then attacked declarer's trump holding by playing ace and another club. Declarer ruffed with his penultimate trump and ruffed his spade loser in dummy. This position had been reached:

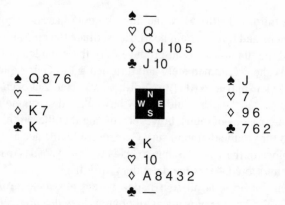

♠ —
♡ Q
♢ Q J 10 5
♣ J 10

♠ Q 8 7 6   ♠ J
♡ —   ♡ 7
♢ K 7   ♢ 9 6
♣ K   ♣ 7 6 2

♠ K
♡ 10
♢ A 8 4 3 2
♣ —

Declarer now ran ♢Q to West's king. The contract was safe on any return. If West played the club king, declarer would ruff in the South hand and cross to ♢J to draw East's last trump.

Have you seen the point of the hand? West should duck when the ◊Q is run to him! Declarer will surely repeat the diamond finesse and West can then force declarer's last trump with the club king. There is no diamond entry to dummy now and East will score his last trump.

On now to the 1996 Cap Volmac World Top Tournament, played in Holland. All sixteen pairs invited to the event were world class, although you would scarcely have guessed it from declarer's line of play on this deal:

Love All
Dealer West

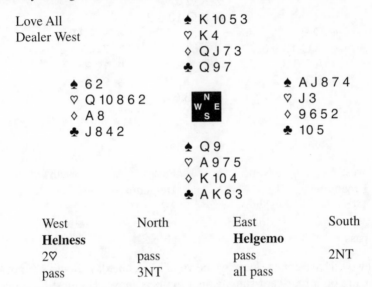

	♠ K 10 5 3
	♥ K 4
	◊ Q J 7 3
	♣ Q 9 7

♠ 6 2　　　　　　　　　♠ A J 8 7 4
♥ Q 10 8 6 2　　　　　♥ J 3
◊ A 8　　　　　　　　　◊ 9 6 5 2
♣ J 8 4 2　　　　　　　♣ 10 5

♠ Q 9
♥ A 9 7 5
◊ K 10 4
♣ A K 6 3

West	North	East	South
Helness		**Helgemo**	
2♥	pass	pass	2NT
pass	3NT	all pass	

Tor Helness led ♥2, playing third and fifth leads. Suppose you had been the declarer. How would you have played the contract?

Declarer rose with dummy's king of hearts and Geir unblocked the jack, an essential move. From the bidding declarer could place one of the missing aces with West, the other with East. The hearts appeared to be 5-2, if the opening lead could be trusted. In that case declarer might need to play first on the suit where West held the ace.

Since three diamond tricks would give declarer the contract if the club suit produced four tricks, you might expect him to play on diamonds first. No, he called for a low spade, perhaps judging that East was less likely to put in the ace of this suit. Wrong! Geir rose with the spade ace and cleared partner's hearts. The contract was now one down.

How did you decide to play the contract? The best idea is to play low from dummy on the heart lead, allowing East's jack to win. No return can harm you.

If East plays back another heart he will have no heart to play when he takes the spade ace.

The next deal comes from the 1999 Blue Ribbon pairs, played in Boston. Geir sat East, partnered by Dick Freeman.

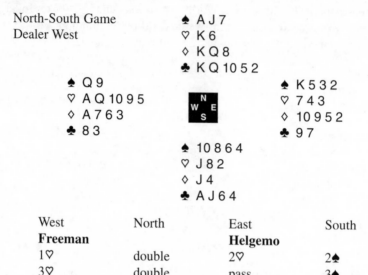

North-South Game — ♠ A J 7
Dealer West — ♡ K 6
◊ K Q 8
♣ K Q 10 5 2

♠ Q 9 — ♠ K 5 3 2
♡ A Q 10 9 5 — ♡ 7 4 3
◊ A 7 6 3 — ◊ 10 9 5 2
♣ 8 3 — ♣ 9 7

♠ 10 8 6 4
♡ J 8 2
◊ J 4
♣ A J 6 4

West	North	East	South
Freeman		**Helgemo**	
1♡	double	2♡	2♠
3♡	double	pass	3♠
pass	4♠	all pass	

West would have gone at least two down in 3♡ doubled, so South's removal of the double on a four-card suit was not the best move. He must have read North's double as a game-try in spades, rather than showing extra strength. The spade game was a poor one, but with the trump suit lying as it did, careful defence was needed.

Freeman led ♣8 and declarer won in hand with the jack. He then played a trump to dummy's jack. Suppose you had been East. How would you have defended?

If you win with the king the contact can no longer be defeated. Partner does not have a singleton club, so no ruff is available there. Suppose you return a heart instead, dislodging dummy's king. Declarer can simply knock out the diamond ace, leaving dummy's ♠7 to deal with a third round of hearts.

It was quite likely that West had started with a singleton club (and perhaps 2-6-4-1 shape). Geir saw that he could beat the contract in any case, by ducking the king of trumps. Declarer played the king of diamonds next. Freeman won with the ace and continued accurately with ace and another heart. Declarer crossed to the jack of diamonds and ruffed his last heart. He then played the ace of trumps, dropping West's queen.

Although declarer now held ♠108 against Geir's ♠K5, the contract could not be made. If he cashed dummy's ◇Q before crossing to a club to knock out the trump king, Geir would be able to force declarer with a diamond. If he left ◇Q in place, Geir would be able to lock declarer in the dummy when he won with the trump king. One down either way!

Our last hand in this chapter is included by way of light relief (we sensed you were feeling weary). Geir and Tor Helness, the eventual winners, faced Zia and Andrew Robson in the 1998 Macallan Pairs.

North-South Game
Dealer South

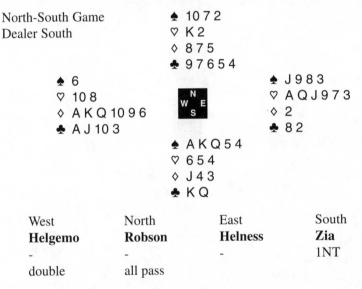

♠ 10 7 2
♡ K 2
◇ 8 7 5
♣ 9 7 6 5 4

♠ 6   ♠ J 9 8 3
♡ 10 8   ♡ A Q J 9 7 3
◇ A K Q 10 9 6   ◇ 2
♣ A J 10 3   ♣ 8 2

♠ A K Q 5 4
♡ 6 5 4
◇ J 4 3
♣ K Q

West	North	East	South
Helgemo	**Robson**	**Helness**	**Zia**
-	-	-	1NT
double	all pass		

Geir's preferred signalling methods in defence are to encourage/discourage on partner's lead and to give count when following suit or discarding. Zia ended in 1NT doubled and Geir ran his diamond suit. Helness pitched ♣8 first, showing an even number of clubs but no interest in the suit. His second discard was the jack of spades. He would scarcely have wasted this card if he had tricks to take or establish in spades, so again this showed an even number of spades and discouraged the suit.

When Geir's diamonds ran out (quite a while later!) he cashed the ace of clubs. This was to cater for partner's ♣8 being a singleton. He then made the indicated switch to hearts. Helness claimed the remaining tricks and Zia was seven down for a penalty of 2000.

16
Imaginative Deception in Defence

Top-class defenders hate to give declarer an easy ride. By disguising their holdings – refusing to take their high cards at the first opportunity, or following with a higher card than is necessary – it is often possible to give declarer a losing option.

On this deal, from a 1993 pairs tournament in Oslo, Geir false-carded in the trump suit to offer declarer a losing alternative.

Game All
Dealer East

	♠ A Q 6 4	
	♡ K 7 3	
	◇ 10 7 3	
	♣ K 10 6	
♠ 10 7 2		♠ J 9 5 3
♡ Q J 8		♡ A 4
◇ Q 9		◇ K J 6 5
♣ 9 8 5 4 2		♣ Q J 7
	♠ K 8	
	♡ 10 9 6 5 2	
	◇ A 8 4 2	
	♣ A 3	

West	North	East	South
Helgemo		**Helness**	
-	-	1◇	1♡
pass	2◇	pass	2♡
pass	3♡	all pass	

Geir led ◇Q, which was allowed to win. The ◇9 continuation was covered by the 10, jack and ace. Declarer's next move was to lead the nine of trumps. Geir covered with the jack and declarer ducked in the dummy, correctly placing the ace with the opening bidder.

Geir's ♣9 switch ran to the ace and declarer now led the two of trumps. The key moment of the deal had been reached. You can see what would happen if Geir followed with the eight. Declarer would duck in the dummy and the bare ace would come from East. The diamond king would then be the defenders' last trick. If a fourth diamond was played, declarer could overruff West's queen with dummy's king. On any other return, the king of trumps would draw West's queen and the contract would be made.

Unwilling to accept this outcome, Geir false-carded the queen on the second round of trumps. It now seemed to declarer that West held Q-J doubleton to East's A-8-4. He called for dummy's king of trumps, losing to the bare ace. The king of diamonds took the next trick and a fourth round of diamonds brought a smile to Geir's ♥8. The contract was one down.

We head for the 1991 Norwegian Teams final now, where Geir's defence on the following deal won the Norske Bank Brilliancy Prize. His somewhat over-imaginative opening lead appeared to have misfired but see what happened next.

East-West Game	♠ Q J 6		
Dealer East	♥ 7 6 4 2		
	◊ Q J		
	♣ K Q J 10		

♠ A 10 9 5 2	♠ 7 4 3
♥ J 10	♥ A 8
◊ 8	◊ K 9 5 4
♣ A 8 6 5 4	♣ 9 7 3 2

♠ K 8
♥ K Q 9 5 3
◊ A 10 7 6 3 2
♣ —

West	North	East	South
Helgemo	**Thomassen**	**Fanavoll**	**Hantveit**
-	-	pass	1♥
1♠	3♥	pass	4◊
pass	4♥	all pass	

Geir led ♣4 (we were all 21 years old once upon a time!) and appeared to have chosen the wrong moment when dummy appeared. Declarer won with dummy's king, throwing a diamond. He then continued with a trump to the queen, the 10 appearing from West. Geir's overcall made it likely that the diamond king would be offside. Since it was also quite possible that West's ♥10 was a singleton, declarer wanted to reach dummy for a second trump lead towards his hand.

Hoping to set up an entry in spades, South advanced the spade king. Geir thwarted this move by allowing the spade king to win. When a second spade was played, Geir went in with the ace. Some defenders would switch to the singleton diamond now, hoping that partner held the ace. Geir had something better in mind, a defence that might well succeed even if East's diamond honour was only the king.

Foreseeing the line that declarer would follow, Geir exited with the ace of clubs! South ruffed and paused to reconstruct the West hand. If West's shape was 5-2-1-5, a second round of trumps from hand would bring in the contract; but surely West would have led his singleton diamond then, rather than risk the underlead of an ace? Concluding that West's shape must be 5-1-2-5 and that ♡10 had been a singleton, declarer aimed once more to reach the dummy. A low diamond to the Q-J seemed to be a good idea.

Helge Hantveit has since changed his views on the matter. East won with the king and gave Geir a diamond ruff. The ace of trumps was the setting trick and declarer had gone down when the diamond king was onside and trumps were 2-2!

Declarer had ample material to make his contract on the next deal, too, from the 2000 Norwegian Premier League. He took one step off the beaten path, however, and a false card from Geir then led him right into the bushes.

Love All
Dealer North

```
                  ♠ 10 7 4 3
                  ♡ A K 3
                  ◇ 10 7
                  ♣ Q J 9 2
   ♠ K Q 5                        ♠ A 9 8 6 2
   ♡ 7 6 2              N         ♡ J 5
   ◇ Q J 4          W     E       ◇ A 8 6 5
   ♣ K 10 8 7          S          ♣ 6 3
                  ♠ J
                  ♡ Q 10 9 8 4
                  ◇ K 9 3 2
                  ♣ A 5 4
```

West	North	East	South
Helgemo		**Austberg**	
-	pass	pass	1♡
pass	3♡	all pass	

Geir led a trump (which, incidentally, is the only lead to defeat *four* hearts). Declarer won East's jack with the queen and played a club to the queen. He should now have led a diamond, preparing for a ruff in that suit. Instead, he returned to the ace of clubs. On this trick Geir dropped the 10, to create the illusion that clubs were 3-3. When declarer played a third round of clubs, the deception was unmasked. Geir played the 8 and East ruffed.

The defence needed to play trumps now, to prevent a diamond ruff. Since Per Erik Austberg had no more trumps, he underled the spade ace in an effort to put his partner on lead. Geir won with the queen and returned a second round of trumps to dummy's ace. A diamond to the king was followed by a second round of diamonds. When Geir won with the jack and played a third round of trumps, the contract was one down.

Many a battle is fought over a long side suit in dummy. All eyes were on dummy's club suit when the next deal arose in a 1998 mixed pairs tournament in Norway's Kristiansand. Geir was partnered by Signy Johansen.

```
Love All              ♠ 8 7 5
Dealer South          ♡ 8
                      ◊ K 9 3
                      ♣ K J 10 9 8 2
         ♠ Q J 9                      ♠ 10 6 4 2
         ♡ K J 5 2          N         ♡ Q 10 7 4
         ◊ Q 10 6       W       E     ◊ J 8 4
         ♣ A 6 5           S         ♣ Q 7
                      ♠ A K 3
                      ♡ A 9 6 3
                      ◊ A 7 5 2
                      ♣ 4 3
```

West	North	East	South
Johansen		**Helgemo**	
-	-	-	1NT
pass	3NT	all pass	

A heart lead would have found partner 'at home', but Johansen chose the safer pairs lead of ♠Q. Declarer won with the ace and played a club to the jack. There was no time for thought, but Geir allowed this card to hold! He knew that declarer held the king of spades and that two clubs and two spades would not be enough to beat the contract. There was an obvious risk that West had started with ace doubleton in the club suit. If you don't like taking risks, bridge is not the game to play!

Declarer returned to his hand with the ace of diamonds and played a second round of clubs to the 10. When Geir won with the queen and returned a spade, South won with the king and West unblocked the jack. Declarer was able to set up a third diamond trick for himself but that was still two down and a top to East-West. Some tables had made the contract on a spade lead. Others had gone one down on a heart lead or switch.

The next deal arose in the 2000 Norwegian Premier League, in a match played in Oslo. Geir, defending in the West seat, could see at an early stage that he had no escape from a squeeze. By discarding in an inventive way, he deprived a careless declarer of his spoils.

```
North-South Game          ♠ A J 6 4
Dealer South              ♡ A J 9 6
                          ◇ 8 4
                          ♣ K 5 3
        ♠ K 10 9 8 2                        ♠ 7 5
        ♡ K               ┌─────┐           ♡ 8 5 2
        ◇ Q 6             │ N   │           ◇ A J 10 9 5 3
        ♣ Q 10 9 7 2      │W   E│           ♣ J 6
                          │  S  │
                          └─────┘
                          ♠ Q 3
                          ♡ Q 10 7 4 3
                          ◇ K 7 2
                          ♣ A 8 4
```

West	North	East	South
Helgemo		**Austberg**	
-	-	-	1♡
1♠	2NT (1)	3◇	3♡
pass	4♡	all pass	

(1) Sound, 4-card raise in hearts.

With both major-suit kings onside, there were eleven tricks readily available. Since Geir held the sole guard in both black suits, a twelfth trick should have come from a simple squeeze.

Geir led the queen of diamonds, overtaken with the ace. Declarer won the diamond return and led the 10 of trumps, picking up West's king. Trumps were drawn in two further rounds and declarer then led the queen of spades, covered by the king and ace. Declarer cashed the jack of spades and ruffed a spade in his hand. This was the end position:

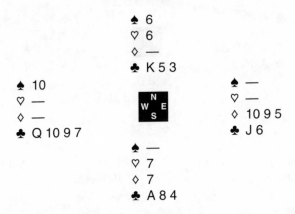

```
                    ♠ 6
                    ♡ 6
                    ◊ —
                    ♣ K 5 3
    ♠ 10                              ♠ —
    ♡ —             ┌─────┐           ♡ —
    ◊ —             │  N  │           ◊ 10 9 5
    ♣ Q 10 9 7      │W   E│           ♣ J 6
                    │  S  │
                    └─────┘
                    ♠ —
                    ♡ 7
                    ◊ 7
                    ♣ A 8 4
```

What would most defenders do when ◊7 appears on the table? They would throw a club, delaying the awful moment as long as possible. Declarer would ruff in dummy, return to the club ace, and cash his last trump, forcing West to abandon one of his guards.

Geir tried something different. When ◊7 was led, he threw his last spade! Since West was not under any pressure at this stage, the half-asleep declarer assumed that he must hold another spade. He subsequently threw dummy's ♠6 away and ended with only eleven tricks for a very bad score.

Perhaps you are tempted to dismiss such a deception with 'How ridiculous. No declarer would fall for that.' There are two retorts we might make in that case. Firstly, a real-life Premier League declarer did fall for it. Secondly, no-one will make such a mistake if you do not offer them the opportunity!

Sometimes both defenders can tell at an early stage that declarer is destined to make the contract. Don't give up! Just look how Geir and his partner, Ole Berset, conjured a way for declarer to go down on this deal from the 1990 European junior championship in Neumünster, Germany:

North-South Game
Dealer South

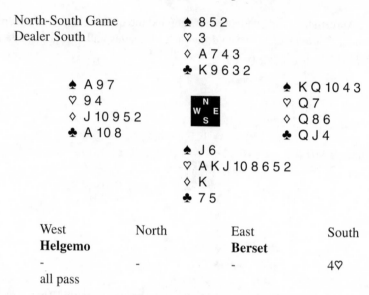

♠ 8 5 2
♡ 3
◊ A 7 4 3
♣ K 9 6 3 2

♠ A 9 7
♡ 9 4
◊ J 10 9 5 2
♣ A 10 8

♠ K Q 10 4 3
♡ Q 7
◊ Q 8 6
♣ Q J 4

♠ J 6
♡ A K J 10 8 6 5 2
◊ K
♣ 7 5

West	North	East	South
Helgemo		**Berset**	
-	-	-	4♡
all pass			

Geir led the jack of diamonds, won with the king. The ace and king of trumps brought down the queen and with the ace of clubs onside there now seemed to be no possible chance of declarer going down. However...

When declarer played a third round of trumps Geir discarded ♣10. On the next two rounds of trumps Berset threw ♣4 and ♣J. Declarer's prospects in the club suit seemed to be rising with each trick that was played. Hoping for more of the same, he tried a sixth round of trumps. No, the defenders seemed to be bored with throwing clubs. They both discarded a spade.

Unable to defer the moment much longer, declarer at last played a club. Geir followed with the eight and – thanks to the earlier discards of the jack and 10 – declarer now had an apparent guess whether to play the king or the nine. His eventual choice was the nine and he gone down in a cold contract.

Perhaps you are thinking, once again, that it was a silly hand and no reasonable declarer would fall for it. Remember the points we made before. An international player – albeit a junior international – *did* fall for the deception at the table. Also, you lose nothing by attempting such trickery. If instead you sit back and do nothing, declarer will chalk up his cold contract anyway. Geir's last word on that deal? 'Hands like this make me wish I was a junior again!'

On the very first deal that Geir played at senior world championship level he picked up these cards, facing USA:

♠ J 8
♡ K 8 6
♦ A 10 9 8 2
♣ K 10 8

The American North opened 1♣, Helness passed, and South responded 1♠. After a pass by Geir, North rebid 4♣. This showed a raise of spades to the game level, along with a club control. South signed off in 4♠ and it was Geir to find a lead. What card would you have chosen as your first in a world championship? Geir led ♦10! This proved to be the full deal:

Love All   ♠ K Q 6 4
Dealer North   ♡ A 10
                            ♦ K 6 5
                            ♣ A Q 9 4

♠ J 8   ♠ A 10
♡ K 8 6   N   ♡ J 9 7 3 2
♦ A 10 9 8 2   W   E   ♦ 7 3
♣ K 10 8   S   ♣ 7 6 3 2

                            ♠ 9 7 5 3 2
                            ♡ Q 5 4
                            ♦ Q J 4
                            ♣ J 5

West	North	East	South
Helgemo	**Weichsel**	**Helness**	**Levin**
-	1♣	pass	1♠
pass	4♣	pass	4♠
all pass			

Levin won the diamond lead with the queen and played a trump to the king and ace. Helness returned his remaining diamond to partner's ace and Geir now led ♦2 for the ruff. This was a McKenney signal, asking for the return of the lower-ranking side suit – clubs instead of hearts. This may have seemed somewhat surprising to Helness, in view of the dummy's holdings. A heart switch would have given declarer a guess for the contract, however. Helness respected his partner's decision and switched to a club. The contract could not now be made. Levin could score three club tricks but East's ♣7 would guard the fourth round.

How did Geir find this devastating opening lead? His ♣K appeared to be badly placed, with the clubs bid over him, and this suggested an aggressive opening lead. Underleading an ace is always dangerous. The time to risk it is when the opponents' values lie mainly to your left. Here it was likely that dummy would hold around 18 points for his game raise; East might hold nearer to 6 points. If dummy went down with K-J and partner held the queen, declarer was likely to misguess. Even if dummy's king was declarer's only asset in the suit, he might not be willing to commit the card.

A hidden benefit of such underleads is that they may cause declarer to misread where other honour cards lie. That was the case on this deal from the 1998 Cap Gemini Pairs:

```
North-South Game        ♠ A K J 9
Dealer South            ♥ Q J 9 7
                        ◇ Q J 10 6
                        ♣ A
        ♠ Q 4 3                         ♠ 8 5
        ♥ A 10 4          N             ♥ K 5 3 2
        ◇ 7            W     E          ◇ K 4
        ♣ K J 8 7 3 2      S            ♣ Q 10 9 5 4
                        ♠ 10 7 6 2
                        ♥ 8 6
                        ◇ A 9 8 5 3 2
                        ♣ 6
```

West	North	East	South
Helgemo	**Jansen**	**Helness**	**Westerhof**
-	-	-	pass
1♣	double	1♥	2◇
double	redouble	3♣	3◇
4♣	5◇	all pass	

Geir's second-round double was a Support Double, showing three-card support for partner's hearts. South arrived in five diamonds and Geir led ♥4. Such leads are always risky, as we have mentioned, and should not to be attempted on a wide scale. Here dummy was known to be strong and partner had bid hearts. Let's go for it!

Geir led ♥4 and the queen was played from dummy. If an ace underlead can be ruled out, East does best to withhold the king. Helness put on his king, nevertheless. He could see from the power in the dummy that the game would be an easy make if declarer held the heart ace.

At Trick 2 Helness returned a low trump. Look at the position from declarer's point of view now. East apparently holds the ace and king of hearts. There are only eighteen points out between the East and West hands and West opened the bidding. He must surely hold the remaining 11 points, including the king of trumps. Westerhof soon had his ace of trumps on the table. The king refused to drop and a seemingly cold game had been defeated.

A further hidden benefit of underleading aces every now and again is that you acquire a reputation for such trickiness. Declarers may believe that you have underled an ace when you have not!

Geir's own reputation for trickery paid dividends on this deal played against Italy in the 1997 Bermuda Bowl:

North-South Game	♠ A Q 9
Dealer North	♥ K 5 3 2
	◊ J
	♣ A Q 8 6 2

♠ 10 7		♠ J 8
♥ Q 10 6	N W E S	♥ A 8 7 4
◊ K 10 9 8 5 4		◊ 7 6 2
♣ 9 4		♣ J 10 7 5

♠ K 6 5 4 3 2
♥ J 9
◊ A Q 3
♣ K 3

West	North	East	South
Helgemo	**Versace**	**Helness**	**Lauria**
-	1♣	pass	1♠
pass	2♥	pass	2NT
pass	3♥	pass	3♠
pass	4♣	pass	4◊
pass	4♥	pass	4NT
pass	5♠	pass	6♠
all pass			

North's 2♡ rebid was artificial. Spades were agreed as trumps and one cue-bid was made in each of the side suits. Geir found the only lead to cause declarer a problem. He led ♡10!

If the lead was a singleton, or from 10-x, the slam was doomed. Since declarer held the nine himself, he had to assume that West had underled either the ace or queen. He had to decide whether West was more likely to lead the ten from A-10-x or Q-10-x.

If West had his mind on deception, considering an underlead of the heart ace, it might well occur to him to choose a tricky ten from A-10-x. From Q-10-x, with no deception in mind, it would be more natural to lead low. Nobody except Lauria knows exactly what went through his mind, but eventually he called for dummy's king. Helness won with the ace and returned a heart for one down. The slam was made at the other table and that was 17 IMPs for Norway.

Would declarer have misguessed if ♡6 had been led? We don't think so!